RESCUING EDEN

PRESERVING AMERICA'S HISTORIC GARDENS

RESCUING EDEN

PRESERVING AMERICA'S HISTORIC GARDENS

PHOTOGRAPHS BY CURTICE TAYLOR

TEXT BY CAROLINE SEEBOHM

THE MONACELLI PRESS

CONTENTS

INTRODUCTION

America's private gardens have been threatened for more than a century. Many eighteenth- and early-nineteenth-century gardens disappeared when the owners moved or died. At the end of the nineteenth century, the newly rich industrial barons created lavish estates on a scale that rivaled the great gardens of Europe. But by the mid-twentieth century, when wars, economic depressions, and social upheavals swept the continent, these luxurious private palaces became less and less sustainable, and much of America's rich garden heritage was destroyed. In Britain, the National Trust was founded in 1895 to protect and preserve the country's architectural and horticultural legacy, but no such institution emerged in the United States. Creeping development, urban sprawl, and increasingly mobile populations crushed the life out of hundreds of once-loved and carefully tended gardens. Thus the brilliant work of landscape designers, architects, and horticulturalists that flourished during their early stewardship of American open space was lost forever.

But not all have disappeared. This book celebrates those that have been rescued from the brink of extinction and those that have been heroically preserved by their owners and then opened to the public. These once-endangered landscapes, thanks to a few groups of fervent garden-saviors, are now accessible to everyone and serve as living, flourishing pleasure grounds for historians, botanists, horticulturists, and garden lovers all over the world.

The gardens were selected for the dramatic value of their original creation and rescue and their historical and horticultural importance. They range from the wonderful to the woebegone, from grand estates to small suburban plots. The locations range from Kentucky to Oregon, from Texas to New Hampshire, from Detroit to Los Angeles. Some are old, some new. Some designers are famous, others unsung. Each garden has its own individual character, and each place has been brought back from the brink through a combination of imagination and dedication. These fortunate few have then been subjected to the equally complex protocols that are required to open them to the public.

Many stories are of gardens that barely escaped oblivion. Years of neglect, deterioration, or encroaching development had left them virtually nonexistent. But before they reverted entirely to nature, they left traces of their past—an old rosebush, fragments of a stone path, a rusted gate, a cluster of overgrown boxwoods. Garden archeologists, botanists, artists, and horticulturists were called in to dig, research, pore over clues as though uncovering the pharoahs' tombs in ancient Egypt. Some gardens were recorded in memoirs, diaries, plant logs, or old photographs that have survived. A corner of a painting, surprisingly, became the critical element in restoring the eighteenth-century William Paca Garden in Annapolis, Maryland. With almost all records lost, restorers studied Charles Willson Peale's portrait of William Paca, painted in 1772, and used the

Above: Rear elevation of the Bartram house, with rubble stone columns from the site.

Right: Path along the Schuylkill River.

artist's minuscule representation of the garden to recreate the design. Through luck, good scholarship, and prescience, or all three, an obscure or unacknowledged document often provided the essential ingredient for the restoration of a garden.

Is it possible that the oldest living botanical garden in the United States could ever have been under threat? Bartram's Garden in Philadelphia was founded in the 1720s by John Bartram. An English Quaker of humble birth and no academic training, Bartram became so successful as a plantsman in England that in 1765 he was appointed Royal Botanist to King George III. But it was in the colonies that he made his name and fortune. Coming to America in the 1730s, he was indefatigable in searching out unclassified plants, trees, and flowers up and down the Eastern Seaboard. Some he shipped home and others he planted in his own backyard on the Schuylkill River. This modest botanical garden soon became famous worldwide. John and his son William created and classified a collection of more than two hundred native North American plants that has never been surpassed. John Bartram died in 1777. In 1783, the family produced the first plant catalog in America, the precursor to Burpees and all the other catalogs we receive in the mail today.

After the Bartram family died out, the garden struggled to survive. Rescue finally came in the form of Philadelphia City Councilman Thomas Meehan, who in 1891 persuaded the City of Philadelphia to acquire the garden and open it to the public. Thus Bartram's Garden became part of the city's Fairmount Park. Today, it belongs to the park and is operated by the John Bartram Assocation, with invaluable support from the Philadelphia

Committee of the Garden Club of America and the West Chester Garden Club. John Bartram, that tough old adventurer and lover of plants, would surely be gratified that his obsession is, after all, recognized as an essential contribution to the environmental history of his adopted country.

City gardens are almost always at risk. Real estate development, that bane of open-space lovers, is not the only enemy. Neglect, politics, and lack of money all combine to make the urban garden an endangered species. New York City's Conservatory Garden is a triumphant example of survival against extreme odds. In 1982, choked with garbage, blanketed in weeds, darkened by huge overgrown hedges, it was considered one of the most dangerous spots in Central Park. Gradually, after an enormous effort spearheaded by the New York arm of the Garden Club of America, funds began to roll in from Rockefeller Center, The Central Park Conservancy, and other generous local donors. Under the direction of landscape designer Lynden Miller, and Central Park's leading light, Elizabeth Barlow Rogers, the Conservatory Garden today is one of the most popular and beloved open-air destinations in New York City.

On a much smaller scale, another city garden claims an equally miraculous rescue. On the State Capitol Mall in St. Paul, Minnesota, is a garden that visitors might not even notice, but it is an important historical site. It is the Minnesota Woman Suffrage Garden, created in 1999 to salute the women of Minnesota who fought to gain the right to vote in the late nineteenth century. The garden in its original form failed. The soil was not nutritious enough to support the plants; the windy site made it difficult for anything to thrive; its sunny location made excessive demands on watering; maintenance was prohibitive. Very soon the original thirty-two beds disappeared under a tangle of weeds. After five years of intensive fundraising, thanks to the Ross Group and the Saint Paul Garden Club, the garden was reinvented with

Left: Conservatory Garden, New York.

Above: View of Philadelphia from Bartram's Garden.

drifts of sturdy plants replacing the high-maintenance beds. Now this powerful little garden presents a proud memorial both to the women warriors of Minnesota and to their descendants, the local supporters who saved it from extinction.

Some threatened gardens have experienced less drastic makeovers. In 1988, Frank Cabot, a self-described "horticultural enthusiast," and his wife, Anne, visited the Ruth Bancroft Garden in Walnut Creek, California. This garden, formerly part of a fruit farm specializing in Bartlett pears, was famous for its succulents collected by Ruth Bancroft, a keen gardener and plantswoman. With Lester Hawkins, co-owner of Western Hills Nursery, helping with the layout, Mrs. Bancroft created a stunning and rare landscape, its originality, beauty, and water-conserving ingenuity garnering much admiration from gardeners and botanists all over the country.

Cabot was shocked to learn that, although Ruth Bancroft was by then in her eighties, there were no plans to preserve this magical place. It was then that the seed, as it were, was planted. The Cabots decided to initiate the journey that became, in 1989, the Garden Conservancy, a nonprofit organization whose mission would be to preserve important American gardens for the benefit of the public. Since then the Garden Conservancy has supported, encouraged, and revived over one hundred gardens in America. Some become specified "preservation gardens," which means long-term involvement in the development of the garden. The Garden Conservancy also offers consultations and preparation of easement programs, along with other professional help. Its popular annual program of "Open Days" has made private gardens accessible to thousands of enthusiasts all over the country. Anyone who bites into a Bartlett pear should give a nod to the vision of Ruth Bancroft and Frank Cabot, whose serendipitous meeting led to such a happy result for the garden history of America.

The other organization that has transformed the look of the American domestic landscape is the Garden Club of America. This venerable nonprofit organization was founded in 1913 by a group of dedicated women who passionately loved gardens and wished to preserve them. Originating even earlier, in 1904, when Elizabeth Price Martin founded the Garden Club of Philadelphia, the idea was to form regional clubs, whose members would inspire their own local communities to work for the rescue and preservation of what they rightly regarded as a vital element of their country's young history.

The Garden Club of America, with two hundred local garden clubs operating today, has become the archivist of record for America's great gardens, both lost and found. In the late nineteenth century, the club's leaders, aware of their responsibility as garden historians, commissioned their members all across the country to record their gardens with glass lantern slides. This astonishing resource—410 lantern slides of 626 gardens—is now in the Smithsonian Institution's Archives of American Gardens. Without those images, the history of some of this country's finest gardens would be lost forever. But the Garden Club of America isn't just about its archives. It is more vital today than it ever was, providing scholarships, prizes, and fellowships for environmental, horticultural, and community agendas, as well as funding significant garden restoration and preservation projects through its prestigious annual Founders Fund.

Inspired by these pioneer organizations, local conservancies, clubs, garden historians, and private individuals throughout America's cities, towns, and villages have come together over the years, not only to identify and preserve their treasures at home, but also to share them with the public. What if Bartram's Garden had become a barren field? What if the Conservatory Garden in Central Park had been left to ruin? What if all the gardens in this book had been turned into dead land or parking lots?

This book celebrates just some of the survivors, with gratitude to the organizations, planners, and volunteers who have stepped up to reveal for future generations a prospect of America's heritage that, with love and nature's help, will last forever.

Above: Prickly pear cacti (left)
and a flowering Trichocereus
in the Bancroft Garden.

MIDDLETON PLACE

CHARLESTON, SOUTH CAROLINA

The Middleton lineage goes back to Edward Middleton, who emigrated from England to South Carolina in 1678 and built a place near Charleston called The Oaks. In 1741 his grandson Henry married Mary Williams, only daughter and heir of John Williams, a rich landowner and civic leader, and the two established Middleton Place on Williams land on the banks of the Ashley River.

At that time, wealthy families were beginning to emulate the great eighteenth- and nineteenth-century English and French gardens they visited on their tours of Europe. There are no records of Henry Middleton visiting France, but like other American cultural explorers of the period, he surely grasped the intentions of great garden designers such as Le Nôtre, for whom the formal allées, the meticulously plotted vistas, and the symmetrical parterres rolling out from the courtyards of the great French palaces were the ideal.

The garden at Middleton Place was laid out in a triangular form, comprising the entrance gate, a reflecting pool, and the main axis running through the house to the terraced lawns sloping down to the river. Trees, formal gardens, extensive paths, a lake, and arbors, were all aligned with the base of the triangle. Sundials, statues, and canals punctuated the spaces.

Opposite: Aerial view of the lawn terraces rippling down to reflecting ponds and the Ashley River beyond.

Right: Spring azaleas frame a classical statue.

After Mary died in 1761, Middleton returned to The Oaks, giving Middleton Place to his son Arthur. Arthur's son, the second Henry Middleton, followed the family tradition of public service, but also focused on enhancing his grandfather's legacy. Advised by the famous French botanist André Michaux, he introduced many new plants into the gardens, including the first camellia in the United States.

The Civil War was not kind to Middleton Place. In early 1865, following the fall of Charleston, a detachment of the 56th New York Volunteers occupied the property, and they burned the main house and both adjacent buildings, or "flankers." The south flanker suffered the least damage and was eventually rebuilt.

This calamity ushered in a long and sad drought—a ruined house, abandoned gardens, a subsequent earthquake, a family dispossessed. It was not until 1925 that

13

J. J. Pringle Smith, a Middleton who had inherited the property in 1916, began to bring the place back to life. His wife, Heningham, an expert gardener, began the work of restoring what people were starting to realize was the oldest surviving landscaped garden in North America. It is thought that its abandonment actually saved it: there was no interest in looting or vandalizing what looked like a series of overgrown graveyards.

In 1941 the Garden Club of America recognized the Smiths' work and declared the gardens at Middleton Place "the most interesting and important in America." But the financial situation deteriorated after the Smiths died. Their grandson Charles Duell confronted the fact that without some radical new way of funding it, Middleton Place would one day have to be sold. He created the Middleton Place Foundation, a nonprofit educational trust that would run the house as part of a conglomerate comprising the Middleton Place gardens, house, and plantation stableyards.

Above: Azaleas dominate the spring planting in many parts of the garden.

Opposite: A view through Spanish moss and azaleas to the undulating lawns and urns in front of the house.

Overleaf: A romantic view of the watery north garden looking toward the Ashley River.

This was an inspired idea. Independent of any government or state stewardship, the Middleton Place Foundation has flourished beyond all expectations. Reborn from the ruins, there is now an inn, a restaurant, and a garden center, as well as a house museum in the rebuilt south flanker. No slave quarters remain on the property, but an exhibition in "Eliza's House," a former freedman's cottage built in the vernacular style of a two-family slave house, tells the story of slavery at Middleton Place. Thus visitors to this evocative compound experience a powerful sense of the eighteenth-century world in which the plantation first prospered. As for the gardens, they have been meticulously revived according to Henry Middleton's original plans. While many of the trees and plants have grown enormously over 250 years, and many new plants and shrubs have been introduced, the bones of his gardens are as strong as ever.

MOFFATT-LADD HOUSE AND GARDEN

PORTSMOUTH, NEW HAMPSHIRE

This Federal mansion was built between 1761 and 1763 on the Piscataqua River by John Moffatt, for his son Samuel and his wife, Sarah Catherine. After the Revolution, the house passed to his granddaughter Mary Tufton Haven Ladd, whose son, Alexander Hamilton Ladd, lived there from 1862 until his death in 1900.

The early owners of the property developed the garden behind the house over the years. Sarah Catherine Moffatt planted an English damask rose in 1768, and her brother-in-law General William Whipple planted a few horse chestnuts from Philadelphia in commemoration of his signing of the Declaration of Independence. The rose and one horse chestnut (on the National Register of Historic Trees) remain in the garden today.

Alexander Hamilton Ladd, who was a successful cotton trader, and his wife, Maria, made many major contributions to the garden, including a terraced formal garden, colorful flowerbeds, and trees. Ladd was a keen plantsman who kept careful records, including a detailed diary that has survived, which show how he acquired his plants. After the 1850s, he began to spend half the year in Texas, and the Portsmouth house became a spring and summer place, the garden reflecting the seasons with spring bulbs and fruit trees. He cultivated tulips, at one time mentioning that in a bad winter he lost over 60,000 bulbs.

Opposite: A 300-foot path with grass steps creates an axis through the terraced garden. Arches over the path incorporate architectural elements, including keystones and Gothic points.

Right: An unusual plant trainer supports a climbing rose.

In the late nineteenth century, the port of Portsmouth declined, and the merchant ships were replaced by freight trains that trundled noisily along the banks of the Piscataqua River, just a few hundred yards from the back of Ladd's garden. The peace was gone; it became dangerous to linger along the river. Ladd's children urged him to move away, but he was determined to hold on to his garden. He died there in 1900, and his children inherited it, maintaining it and using it occasionally for family celebrations. Ultimately they acquired their own summer houses, and the property suffered neglect.

According to a recently discovered document in the archives, there was a plan to sell the house and repurpose it as a home for elderly men. Instead, in 1911 the family donated the house and garden to the National Society of the Colonial Dames of America in the state

Left: The rear elevation of the Federal townhouse overlooks the garden; the borders are currently under restoration.

Right: Phlox and yarrow lend vivid midsummer color.

of New Hampshire to be preserved as a museum, complete with family furniture and decorative arts. In 1912 Ernest Bowditch made a plan for restoration of the garden, and that same year the Colonial Dames opened the property to the public. Made a National Historic Landmark in 1968, the Moffatt-Ladd House and Garden celebrated its 250th anniversary in 2013.

Above: The original beehive shed and white-painted fences have been restored.

Opposite: A shady seating area near the grape arbor.

Overleaf: At the lower terrace garden arches and fences give structure to the colorful borders.

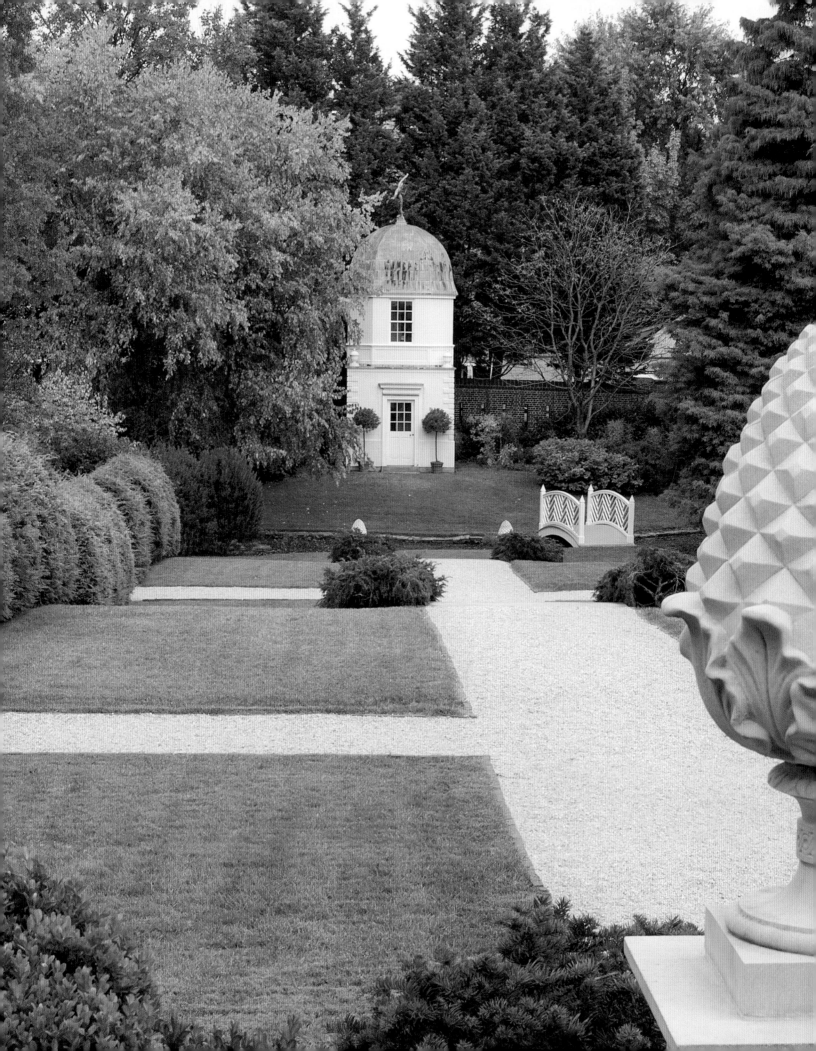

WILLIAM PACA HOUSE AND GARDEN

ANNAPOLIS, MARYLAND

The third quarter of the eighteenth century is often called the Golden Age of Annapolis—a time when prominent citizens made their mark on this colonial seaport by erecting gracious brick homes. The young lawyer William Paca foresaw a life of prosperity and civic responsibility here, and indeed, he would eventually become one of Annapolis's most prominent citizens, a signer of the Declaration of Independence, and later a state senator, governor, and judge. Four days after his marriage to Mary Chew in 1763, he purchased two lots in the center of the city, a total of two acres, and planned accordingly for the life of his family. Paca's Federal mansion is one of the Golden Age's architectural gems.

However, it is the garden that is unique. Paca laid out this two-acre oasis of natural beauty while his house was being built. A Chesapeake falling (sloping) garden, it features a series of four terraces, which were characteristic of colonial gardens in the region. The terraces are bisected by a central allée, with a short flight of limestone steps leading down each slope. The upper garden is divided into four "rooms," each with a different parterre pattern. On the upper terrace, one parterre features heirloom roses while another is planted with flowers typical of the eighteenth century. On the next terrace, the holly parterre and the boxwood parterre preside. Tucked beside them are a kitchen garden and orchard.

Opposite: A pond separates the summer house from the garden itself.

Right: Charles Willson Peale's portrait of William Paca, 1772, includes a glimpse of the summer house and garden.

Beyond the parterres is the Wilderness, which reflects the picturesque style of gardening that became fashionable in England after 1740. Here, paths meander among beds filled with native plants. Central to the Wilderness is the summer house. A two-story white stucco folly with a bell-shaped roof, the summer house serves as a focal point for the garden. On its upper floor the Paca family could view the garden, entertain guests, and catch cool summer breezes. A Chinese Chippendale–style bridge provides a path over the pond to this inviting garden retreat.

Opposite and right: Winding
gravel paths and garden
structures evoke the design of
the original kitchen garden.

But the garden has not existed in this pristine state continuously; in fact, it had been lost
for many years. Paca sold the house in 1780, and the property changed hands several
times during the nineteenth century, often occupied by renters. In 1901 the property was
purchased by a developer and the house transformed into Carvel Hall with the addition
of a multistoried hotel wing. Over the years many feet of fill dirt buried the lower garden
as it was leveled for a parking lot. When the hotel went up for sale in 1965, Historic
Annapolis Inc., founded in 1952 by Anne St. Clair Wright, bought the house. Following
Wright's leadership, the state of Maryland bought the rest of the property, and a major
restoration project began.

Unlike the archival documentation of some rescued gardens, here there was little to go on.
But a portrait of William Paca, painted by Charles Willson Peale in 1772, miraculously
showed a glimpse of the garden in the background. Prompted by the clues provided by this
painting, Historic Annapolis commissioned a total of five archaeological digs between 1967
and 1990. The early investigations confirmed the existence and location of the features in
the painting, and on this basis, restoration began. The foundation of the brick wall surrounding the garden was uncovered, and sloped areas in the wall revealed the location of
the "falls" between the terraces. Landscape architect Laurence Brigham drew plans based

Left: The formal boxwood patterns reflect the original late-eighteenth-century design of the garden.

Opposite: Plantings of heirloom flowers and a Chinese-style bench offer a pleasing resting place.

Overleaf: The summer house terminates the main axis from the house.

on these findings and information drawn from gardening manuals of Paca's time. The earth was shaped to its original contours, the pond was rediscovered, and the natural spring that had once fed the pond bubbled to life when the springhouse foundation was excavated. By 1973 the beds had been filled with plants authentic to Paca's era, garden buildings and waterways had been reconstructed, and the site opened to the public. The restoration of the house stretched on until 1976, when, appropriately enough, it too was opened in time for national bicentennial celebrations. For more than fifty years Historic Annapolis has acted as steward to this magnificent garden, tending the plantings and interpreting the life of the garden and the house through publications, tours, exhibits, and events.

BARNSLEY GARDENS

ADAIRSVILLE, GEORGIA

This garden was originally part of a large estate called Woodlands, founded in 1841 by Godfrey Barnsley, a successful transplant from Liverpool, England, who had made a fortune in the cotton trade. In 1828 he married Julia Scarborough of Savannah and purchased 4,000 acres in northwest Georgia to build her a dream house. It was to be in the Italianate style inspired by the work of the well-known architect and landscape designer Andrew Jackson Downing.

In 1845 after Julia's untimely death, construction on the house stopped. According to legend, Barnsley had a dream in which his wife urged him to complete the project, and finally, in 1858 the lavish sixteen-room mansion and gardens were finished. In 1864 Sherman's armies marched through Georgia, devastating the plantations in their path. Woodlands survived, but Barnsley lost his fortune. He died and was buried at Woodlands in 1873.

His descendants remained on the estate, although they moved into the kitchen wing in 1906, after a tornado destroyed the roof of the main house. In 1942 Woodlands, now renamed Barnsley Gardens and fallen into total disrepair, was auctioned off. At this point Godfrey Barnsley's vision seemed just another Southern phantom.

Opposite and right: The shell of the manor house was stabilized in the 1970s, and the walls now provide a striking frame for the surrounding gardens.

In 1988 Prince Hubertus Fugger, scion of a rich Bavarian family, purchased Barnsley Gardens sight unseen, going on to create the golf resort that now rises spectacularly from the ruins of the plantation house. Clent Coker, who has spent a lifetime researching the Barnsley saga and who established the Barnsley Museum in 1991, worked with Prince Fugger on the gardens, reviving the plans inspired by Downing. Original boxwoods, for decades swallowed up by weeds and vines, were uncovered and trimmed; flowerbeds, paths, and parterres, revealed and restored. Now two hundred varieties of roses bloom as a salute to this fascinating history. Today Barnsley is one of the few antebellum gardens surviving in the South.

Left: Weddings and other celebrations are held amid the ruins of the mansion.

Above: The ruins overlook woodland and boxwood, a touch of romance in this historic landscape.

Left: The formal lawn and gardens to the rear of the house still stand, along with a restored pergola and original trees draped in wisteria.

Above top: The manor house, c. 1880.

Above: The original boxwood design reflected the influence of Andrew Jackson Downing.

Above and right: Ongoing restoration is focused on the formal gardens, the pond, and stone elements that date back to the mid-nineteenth century.

Opposite: Woodland paths wind through the original garden.

SAINT-GAUDENS NATIONAL HISTORIC SITE

CORNISH, NEW HAMPSHIRE

The National Park Service preserves Aspet, the home, studio, and gardens of Augustus Saint-Gaudens, the greatest American sculptor and the central figure of the Cornish Art Colony, a group of artists who gathered in the summers along the Connecticut River below Mount Ascutney.

Saint-Gaudens and his family began to spend summers in Cornish in the mid-1880s, encouraging friends and fellow artists to join them there. The grounds of Aspet include broad lawns stretching to deep woods and a series of gardens closer to the house and the studios. The gardens show the obvious features of a sculptor's taste: a vine-covered colonnade beside his main studio, sculptural pine and hemlock hedges, strategically placed pools and fountains, and statuary from antiquity or created by the sculptor himself. There is also a temple designed in 1905 as a stage set to celebrate the twentieth anniversary of Saint-Gaudens's arrival in Cornish. Today the temple holds the remains of the artist, his wife, and other family members.

The Cornish Art Colony flourished around the property from about 1895 to the 1920s. Lured by the beauty of the valley and mountains of Vermont, writers, painters, sculptors, and dancers flocked to this haven of artistic freedom and were inspired to produce work that in some cases, made their names. Painters Maxfield Parrish, Kenyon Cox, and Thomas Dewing, sculptor Paul Manship, landscape designer Ellen Biddle Shipman, architect and painter Charles Adams Platt, and dancer Isadora Duncan were some of the best-known members of the group.

Opposite: Gilded-bronze cast of *Amor Caritas*, 1898, installed in the atrium court.

Right: Relief of Pan at the end of the exedra.

Overleaf: Tall yew hedges are punctuated with white birch and marble herms.

After Saint-Gaudens's death in 1907, the place lost its raison d'être. Without the sculptor's personal charisma, other artists stopped coming to the area. His widow and son attempted to maintain the property, but money was tight and in 1919 they deeded it to a board of trustees as the nonprofit Saint-Gaudens Memorial, incorporated and chartered by the state of New Hampshire. Gifts from the Metropolitan Museum of Art, friends, and local supporters helped keep the site going, and summer concerts added to the operating funds.

Opposite: The Pan pool is tucked between the Little Studio and the terraced garden. Elephant Ear, popular in the Gilded Age, was first planted by Saint-Gaudens in 1902.

Above: Saint-Gaudens considering the layout of the formal garden.

In 1964 the Saint-Gaudens Memorial donated Aspet to the National Park Service, and the following year it was declared a National Historic Site. The National Park Service is now responsible for maintenance and management of the site, which has expanded into an extensive park with hiking trails through natural areas, while the trustees of the Memorial, led by the Platt family, sponsor musical programs and artist residencies and exhibitions. The studios exhibit maquettes and casts of Saint-Gaudens's best-known works, including the *Diana* from the Stanford White's Madison Square Garden in New York. The original cast of the monument of Civil War Admiral David Farragut is installed in a pavilion on the grounds. Although altered over the years, Saint-Gaudens's garden remains a fine example, with its formal layout and various monuments, of how a sculptor embarks on the design of a domestic landscape. Interestingly, this is the only site in the federal parks system devoted to a visual artist, with a collection of the artist's work on-site.

Top: The Pan pool, thought to be the first garden installed by Saint-Gaudens.

Above: The formal garden enclosed by tall hedges.

Right: Garden elevation of Aspet. The house is named for the French village where Saint-Gaudens's father was born.

Left: Hermes in the formal
garden.

Opposite: Hollyhocks beside
the Little Studio.

BLITHEWOLD GARDENS

BRISTOL, RHODE ISLAND

In 1895 Augustus Van Wickle and his wife, Bessie, commissioned the well-known Beaux-Arts architects Hoppin & Koen to build a large, Queen Anne–style mansion on waterfront land in Bristol. Van Wickle could afford it. He was born into a successful coal-mining family in Hazleton, Pennsylvania. Bessie was the daughter of Ario Pardee, one of Hazleton's richest coal barons, so their marriage was one of those unions blessed with riches on both sides.

Blithewold (Old English for "happy woodland") was the result of Van Wickle's search for a summer residence on the water where he could sail his yacht *Marjorie* (named after his daughter). He and his wife asked the Bristol-born landscape architect John De Wolf, later superintendent of Prospect Park, Brooklyn, to design the landscape of the seventy-acre estate. With Bessie Van Wickle as his avid supporter in the development of the garden, De Wolf annexed thirty-three acres to create display gardens and a "bosquet," as well as a rock garden, a water garden, an enclosed garden, a rose garden, a moon gate, and strategic plantings of specimen trees and shrubs that allowed stunning views across the parkland to Narragansett Bay. The most visited place was the North Garden, a formal parterre planted with colorful flowers, surrounded by low rustic stone walls and edged with boxwood. Greenhouses and a palm house designed for Bessie in 1901 by glass conservatory builders Lord & Burnham were elegant architectural features of the grounds.

Opposite: The modern experimental garden, planted by volunteer horticulturalists, contains plants that are native to Rhode Island.

Right: The marble fountain is the focal point at the base of the double staircase descending from the house to the lawns and garden.

However, a series of tragedies shadowed this happy landscape. In 1898 Augustus was killed by the accidental misfire of his own gun when out skeet-shooting. Five months later, Bessie gave birth to their second daughter, Augustine. In 1901 Bessie married William Leander McKee, a wealthy Boston businessman and old friend of her late husband. McKee and his new family continued to enjoy their summer paradise, until 1906, when Blithewold burned to the ground. Undaunted, the couple immediately built another, much grander mansion. Turning away from the Beaux-Arts tradition, they selected the Boston firm of Kilham & Hopkins, who gave them a stone house in the English style, newly in favor with the Gilded Age gentry.

Left and above: The rustic
stone bridge echoes the stone
of the main house. Water lilies,
water iris, and Joe Pye weed
flourish in the pond.

Left: A moon gate and double borders act as the official entrance to the house and gardens.

Right: Adirondack chairs in front of the house overlook the lawn that descends to the harbor.

Bessie's daughter Marjorie married George Armstrong Lyon in 1914 in the enclosed garden at Blithewold and spent much of her married life enjoying the beautiful landscape created by her mother. During the Depression, the McKees suffered financial reversals and moved full-time to Blithewold, selling off thirty-five acres of the land. They also dismantled a greenhouse and the palm house, citing prohibitive maintenance. After Bessie's death, Marjorie became chatelaine of Blithewold, continuing to develop the gardens. When she died in 1976, she left the estate to the Heritage Trust of Rhode Island, in expectation that the gardens would be preserved and enjoyed by the public forever. But the maintenance costs proved too much for the trust, whose members turned in desperation to a private developer in 1998. His proposal was to privatize the gardens.

A small group of outraged local supporters banded together and raised $650,000 in a few weeks to keep the estate open. In 1999 the group incorporated as Save Blithewold Inc., a nonprofit organization dedicated to keeping the house and garden open to the public, while instituting a sustainable financial plan for the future. Thanks to these efforts, and to deep and meticulously preserved archives, Blithewold and the major elements of De Wolf's original early-twentieth-century design remain intact, including the various pathways, flower and water gardens, trees, and shrubs. Blithewold today offers a window into a world long gone as well as a lesson in continuity.

FLORENCE GRISWOLD MUSEUM

OLD LYME, CONNECTICUT

Probably the most famous artist's garden is Monet's retreat at Giverny, but a lesser-known artist's garden—that of Florence Griswold, in Old Lyme, Connecticut—demonstrates the same kind of free-form palette of color, shape, and texture that characterizes the planting at Giverny.

Florence Ann Griswold was born into a patrician family of governors and jurists, but after her father's death, her mother struggled financially. The girls' school she opened in their house in Old Lyme failed, and the family was reduced to taking in boarders. By 1900 Florence was the last member of her family residing at Griswold House. Her mother and sister Louise had died, and her other sister Adele was sent to live in an institute in Hartford. Florence was left to try to make a living as best she could. What evolved was Florence's great inspiration: a boardinghouse for artists.

It began with painter Henry Ward Ranger, who visited in 1899 and fell in love with the house, the garden, the trees, and the view to the river. The following spring he started a Barbizon-style art colony that soon expanded into one of the best-known centers in the country, with Childe Hassam perhaps its most famous member. The property offered a visual feast to the artist-boarders. Griswold loved to garden, and had a good eye for flowers. Like her English contemporary Gertrude Jekyll, she liked to mass various species together, creating blowsy informal perennial beds that exploded with color: hollyhock, iris, foxglove, heliotrope, and phlox were some of her favorites. The paintings the artists produced during the heyday of the colony are redolent of the inspiration they found in these delightful little landscapes.

Opposite: The rose pergola in May, with peonies in the dappled light that so inspired the visiting artists.

Right: William Chadwick, *On the Piazza*, 1908. Florence Griswold Museum.

During the Depression, Griswold's health began to fail, and she lost much of her income as fewer and fewer artists came up to Old Lyme. In 1936 the Florence Griswold Association was formed to try and stop this decline, intending to maintain the house and garden and hopefully turn it into an art museum. But owing to lack of funds, the estate was sold to Judge Robert McCurdy Marsh, who allowed Griswold to stay in the house until her death in December 1937. Her belongings were quickly sold at auction, and the future looked bleak for the once-thriving property. However, the Florence Griswold Association rallied, and in 1941 the group bought the house back from the

Opposite: A mixture of Griswold's favorite flowers, such as mock orange, coral bells, and aruncus.

Right: *Florence Griswold with Phlox*, c. 1915. Florence Griswold Museum.

Overleaf: The museum's education center was designed to evoke the original barn/ studio on the property.

judge with less than one acre of land. The Florence Griswold Museum opened to the public for summers only in 1947.

From then on, the crisis eased. The Florence Griswold Association and Lyme Historical Society merged, successful fund-raising helped put the museum on a sound footing, and in 1993 it was named a National Historic Landmark. As for the garden, supporters over the years managed to reclaim some of the land that had been lost, and focused on restoring it to its original beauty. Archaeological digs revealed the early outlines of the beds and paths; photographs and paintings done by the original members of the artists' colony helped the restorers replant the flowers Griswold had so loved. In the past few years, new trees, shrubs, heirloom perennials, and native flowers have been added, ensuring that Florence Griswold's brilliant contribution to both gardening and American art will never be forgotten.

CUMMER MUSEUM OF ART AND GARDENS

JACKSONVILLE, FLORIDA

The evolution of this garden could be called "The Story of Three Wives." The patriarch of the family was Wellington Cummer, a successful lumber merchant who moved his family from Michigan to Jacksonville, Florida, in 1896 to start a new and bigger business. He became a pillar of the community, building a large neo-Georgian home on the bank of the St. Johns River. His sons Arthur and Waldo followed their father into the Cummer Lumber Company and, showing admirable filial piety, built homes on either side of their father's mansion.

But in this family it was the wives who made the most lasting contribution to American art and culture. Ada, wife of Wellington, Ninah, wife of Arthur, and Clara, wife of Waldo, turned their attention to the landscaping of their houses and, as befitted their social status, summoned the best-known names in the nation to design their gardens.

The first star to arrive was Ossian Cole Simonds, a well-known landscape designer from the Cummers' home state of Michigan, who envisioned large sweeps of lawn and banks of trees, with stands of live oaks along the riverfront. After he set the scene, so to speak, Thomas Meehan & Sons produced a classical English garden for Arthur and Ninah in 1910. Then came Ellen Biddle Shipman, one of the most famous women gardeners of the twentieth century. In 1931, she designed a glorious Italian garden for Ninah, who by this time had collected Italian garden ornaments as well as hundreds of her beloved azaleas. Shipman gave her client what she wanted: fountains, reflecting pools, carefully sited objects—in short the most authentic Italian garden money could buy.

Opposite: The Italian garden designed by Ellen Biddle Shipman incorporates slender cedars and terracing.

Right: One of the green arches inspired by the Florentine garden Villa Gamberaia frames an Italian fountain.

Not to be outdone, Clara and Waldo brought in their own celebrity designer, William Lyman Phillips—a partner in the Olmsted Brothers firm—who was working on the Fairchild Tropical Garden in Coral Gables at the time. His challenging assignment was to incorporate a large expanse of Ada's grounds, acquired following her death in 1929, with Clara's existing formal gardens, making all blend successfully.

65

Arthur Cummer died in 1943, at which point Ninah began collecting more seriously, this time European and American fine art, which she planned to donate to a museum that would be built "on the property," meaning the land of the combined Cummer holdings. In other words, she would bequeath to the museum the house her husband built, but one of the two remaining Cummer houses would be demolished to make room for the Cummer Gallery of Art, a plan that inevitably threatened the gardens.

Ninah's dream came to fruition at her death in 1958. In 1961 the museum was opened to great fanfare. When Ninah's sister-in-law Clara died, her property was subdivided, and much of Clara and Ada's fabulous shared garden creation was buried under two office buildings and their parking lots. In subsequent years, even Ninah's much-admired gardens lost their luster, and some of their original elements, including the names of their architects, faded into history.

Nevertheless, the bones of the English garden, the water features and statuary from the Italian garden, and the Olmsted garden were not lost forever. A team of dedicated volunteers shepherded the ongoing preservation of the English and Italian gardens, uncovering their unique history and making them an important part of the museum's assets. In 1994, the gallery's name was changed to the Cummer Museum of Art and Gardens, and in 1999 the museum mounted a rehabilitation effort for the English and Italian gardens, using Ninah's original plant logs and other records—miraculously extant. The garden in the most serious jeopardy, the Olmsted garden—"a jungle," said chief curator Holly Keris—was purchased by the museum in 1990, restored, and opened to the public in 2013, two years after the Cummer Gardens were listed on the National Register of Historic Places.

Thanks to commitments from the Jacksonville community and grants from the Bureau of Historic Preservation, Division of Historical Resources, Florida Department of State, assisted by the Florida Historical Commission, the gardens have emerged from obscurity and are open to the public today, almost as dazzling as they were one hundred years ago and providing an unprecedented historical record of the work of some of the nation's most important landscape architects.

Opposite: The statue of Mercury has been reinstalled in the Olmsted garden.

Left: The English garden, with its "breathable" wall, is the oldest part of the garden.

Above: Ninah Cummer in the English garden.

ANNA SCRIPPS WHITCOMB CONSERVATORY

DETROIT, MICHIGAN

This magnificent conservatory, completed in 1904, is the centerpiece of Belle Isle, a park on the Detroit River designed by Frederick Law Olmsted in the 1880s. Those years represented the period of Detroit's apotheosis as the center of the automobile industry, so naturally the most important landscape architect in the country was selected to plan the park. The architect of the conservatory was Prussian-born Albert Kahn, just beginning his illustrious career as designer of massive plants and office buildings for the automobile manufacturers in Detroit, as well as the institutional buildings they endowed and the palatial mansions in which they lived.

In designing the Belle Isle Conservatory, Kahn produced a classical building and a lasting monument to Detroit's place in the world: a gleaming glasshouse sitting on about one acre, with a central dome, where gigantic palms and tropical plants compete to reach the sky. The building has two wings, one for ferns and cacti, the other for countless tropical rarities. Opposite the entrance vestibule is a show house for special floral displays. A lily pond (added later) and perennial borders decorate the exterior landscape.

The conservatory was an immediate success, and for much of the twentieth century visitors came from all over to admire its beauty and its collections. In 1953 its elegant wooden frame was replaced by more durable aluminum. Also in 1953, Anna Scripps Whitcomb, daughter of *Detroit News* founder James E. Scripps, donated her collection of six hundred orchids to the conservatory. In gratitude the conservatory was renamed for her.

Opposite: Trees like the ponytail plant and prickly pear cactus present strange shapes in the cactus and succulent house.

But as Detroit's fortunes fell, so did the conservatory's. The cost of maintaining the glass, the interior climate controls, and the fragile plant materials became increasingly prohibitive. Belle Isle Park also declined. The central Scott Fountain stopped running, trees fell down, canals became clogged, walkways went unweeded. Even the conservatory, still shimmering in the midst of this dishevelment, lost its luster. In February 2014 the Michigan Department of Natural Resources leased the park from the city of Detroit, with a plan to assume maintenance, make major improvements, and restore the park to its former glory.

Above: The collection of ferns brings scholars and visitors to the conservatory all year-round.

Opposite: An early-twentieth-century postcard of the conservatory.

Overleaf: The lily pond outside the conservatory, a more recent addition, features water plants, grasses, and a little cascade.

Horticultural Bldg, Belle Isle, Detroit, Mich.

But the people of Detroit had not been idly standing by during the dark years. In 1972 the nonprofit Friends of Belle Isle was founded to help restore the park. In 1988 the Belle Isle Botanical Society began to focus on maintaining the conservatory's infrastructure and collections. Two more nonprofits also entered the fray: in 2004 the Belle Isle Women's Committee and in 2005 the Friends of the Belle Isle Aquarium. In 2009, these four organizations banded together and, with the help of funding from the Kresge Foundation, the Cultural Alliance for Southeastern Michigan, and the Michigan Nonprofit Association, formed the Belle Isle Conservancy. Thanks to the energy and fund-raising skills of this new community, much work has already been done in the park. The fountain is flowing again. Trees have been pruned. A strong police presence has reduced the traffic problems. The conservatory is being repaired, and the collections attended to. Visitors are coming back, delighted to be able to wander again freely through the tropical gardens of the conservatory. With these tremendous efforts from the state and private citizens, Kahn's inspired creation is regaining its place among Detroit's most historic and glamorous landmarks.

THE FELLS

NEWBURY, NEW HAMPSHIRE

John Milton Hay, born in 1838, became Abraham Lincoln's assistant secretary at the age of twenty-two, and went on to be ambassador to Great Britain and secretary of state under Presidents William McKinley and Theodore Roosevelt. In 1888 he and his wife, Clara Louise Stone, acquired more than a thousand acres of land on the shore of Lake Sunapee. They hired Cleveland-based architect George F. Hammond to design their house in the Colonial Revival style that Hammond favored.

The gardens originate with the Hays' son Clarence who, with his wife, Alice Appleton Hay, turned the estate into a serious horticultural landscape. Inheriting the property on his father's death in 1905, Clarence turned some of the forests and fields into a series of gardens, including lawns, a walled courtyard, and woodland garden. The couple built a 100-foot-long stone wall to frame a perennial border with iris, delphinium, hollyhocks, phlox, and other colorful flowers. More walls and a fountain decorated a rose garden underplanted with annuals. They also created a spectacular rock garden with a stream and lily pool.

In 1960 Clarence and Alice Hay deeded 675 acres of the property, mostly the uncultivated part, to the Society for the Protection of New Hampshire Forests. Clarence died in 1969, and his wife died in 1987, at which point the rest of the estate, including the buildings and gardens, was deeded to the United States Fish and Wildlife Service (USFWS), and named the John Hay National Wildlife Refuge.

The USFWS was not interested in the upkeep of the cultivated part of the estate, and after a series of discussions with them and the New Hampshire Forests Society, an organization called the Friends of the John Hay Wildlife Refuge was formed to support the historic buildings and develop the site for educational purposes. From 1989 to 1992, the members attempted to fulfill their agenda. But the gardens suffered, and in 1991 the Friends approached the Garden Conservancy about their plight, and the Conservancy agreed to help.

Opposite: At its peak in the 1930s, the rock garden boasted more than 600 species of rock and alpine plants.

Right: The urn fountain in the wall of the rose terrace was created between 1924 and 1927.

Above: The original rose
terrace now contains shrub
roses, annuals, and perennials.

Opposite: Construction of
the rock garden in the late
1920s or early 1930s.

Octopus-like, the bureaucracy surrounding the gardens expanded. More departments were called in, including the State Division of Historic Resources, and, along with the USFWS, a new organization was formed, called the Historic Preservation Committee, which in turn produced yet another organism, the Historic Landscape Committee. Gradually this committee made some progress with the gardens. The members began fund raising and found local and national support. Thanks to the Garden Conservancy, volunteer work parties started on the restoration of the various hedges, rose beds, rock garden, and perennial borders, so long in disarray. In the fall of 1995, the Garden Conservancy reported that "40 garden volunteers added a new nursery and plant sales area . . . as well as continuing to renovate the plantings along the entrance drive, improve maintenance of the perennial border, install demonstration plantings on the rose terrace, and stabilize and inventory the rock garden."

Issues with the various federal and state committees led finally to the incorporation in 1997 of the Friends of the John Hay National Wildlife Refuge, which, with the USFWS and the New Hampshire Forests Society, somehow continued to lurch along together for another decade. In 2008 eighty-four acres of the historic buildings and gardens were transferred to The Fells, yet another nonprofit organization, finally freeing the property from the fragile relationships for so long sustained with the federal and state agencies. Thus, after years of frustratingly complex bureaucratic and financial constraints, the gardens are finally restored to their former splendor for the enjoyment of the public.

Above: This statue is known as Hebe, though in a modern interpretation. The steps descend to the gravel entrance court of the house.

Right: This shady woodland walk is part of the original 1909 garden, which is now in the process of restoration.

Overleaf: A romantic vista from the rose terrace across the rock gardens down to Lake Sunapee.

UNTERMYER PARK AND GARDENS

YONKERS, NEW YORK

In the pantheon of great Gilded Age estates in the United States, the Untermyer Gardens take pride of place. The design was the brainchild of lawyer and philanthropist Samuel Untermyer, who bought the 150-acre property, then called Greystone, from former New York governor and presidential candidate Samuel Tilden in 1899.

Untermyer, the son of a Virginia tobacco farmer, was a man of huge ambition for his New York estate, and in 1915 he hired William Welles Bosworth to design his garden. Bosworth was an interesting choice; he was first and foremost an architect, who later moved to Paris and worked on the restoration of the palace of Versailles. But he was also a protégé of the Rockefeller family, for whom he designed the gardens at Kykuit. This convinced Untermyer that Bosworth could do wonders for his own property, and indeed he did.

Belle Epoque grandeur was the theme. A Persian garden, a stairway modeled after the Villa d'Este in Italy, ancient Cipollino marble pillars framing the view of the Hudson River and Palisades, loggias and fountains, all conspired to produce visions of untold pleasures. Bosworth created a gazebo called the Temple of Love with terraces, water features, and a rock garden built by Charles Davite, a Genoese craftsman brought from Italy for the task. A Greek amphitheater (for Isadora Duncan to dance in), rills, reflecting pools, grottoes, mosaics, marble statues by Paul Manship, and flowerbeds tended by sixty gardeners were some of the elements that helped create what even in those days of wealth and excess was claimed to be, in Untermyer's own modest words: "the finest garden in the world."

Opposite: Sphinxes by Paul Manship crown pairs of Cipollino marble columns. Across the lawn is the Temple of the Sky.

Right: Water lilies in the main canal.

But Samuel Untermyer's garden was doomed, like so many others of that sybaritic age, to be consigned to the history books. Untermyer wished to bequeath the gardens to New York State, Westchester County, or the city of Yonkers. But when he died in 1940, none of these entities was prepared, either politically or financially, to take on the maintenance of this overreaching landscape, particularly since a world war was looming and Untermyer, showing a surprising lack of foresight, had not provided an accompanying endowment. In a few short years, Untermyer's proud boast had been translated into "America's greatest forgotten garden."

Opposite: The Temple of Love is poised on a man-made rock formation. Water originally flowed down the face of the stone to the basin below.

Right, top: The original design featured an Italianate stepped vegetable garden. The pavilions are similar to those at Kykuit.

Right: Isadora Duncan and her troupe performed in the amphitheater in 1922.

Overleaf: A crenellated wall shelters the amphitheater.

In 1946 the city of Yonkers agreed to take part of the estate and, after selling much of the land, turned the remaining sixteen acres into a public park. Two years later, the house was razed, and the gardens were minimally maintained. But in 2010, thanks to the leadership of former Yonkers resident Stephen F. Byrns, the Untermyer Gardens began to come back to life. An architect, a former commissioner of the New York City Landmarks Preservation Commission, and a director of the Wave Hill garden in Riverdale, Byrns founded the Untermyer Gardens Conservancy, enlisting the help of Marco Polo Stufano of Wave Hill and Timothy Tilghman, head horticulturist at the Yonkers Parks Department. Their assignment was simple: to raise money and restore as much as possible of what remained of Untermyer's fantastic dream.

In the past five years, a miracle has taken place. The Greek columns still stand. Manship's statues remain. The mosaics in the circular temple and ruined swimming pool still (partially) exist. The rock garden is still a rock garden, now re-exposed. The vista from the garden to the Hudson and Palisades still thrills. As for the rest, gardeners have weeded, cleaned, patched, irrigated, planted, carved, scrubbed, sealed, filled, and uncovered some of the countless garden structures that Bosworth so lavishly dispersed throughout the landscape. The Persian Garden, the amphitheater, and the decorated pavements were all brought back to life. In 2013 the Garden Club of America Founders Fund, at the request of the Irving Garden Club, agreed to help restore the Temple of Love. The work continues.

The Untermyer Gardens will never fully regain the splendor of the early 1900s. What remains is scarred, imperfect, flickering in the sunlight, but still glamorous, like a movie star from the silent era, conveying that indestructible magic to a new generation of admirers.

Above: An open field with a view to the Hudson River will become a wildflower meadow.

Opposite: A pair of ancient Cipollino marble columns terminates the Vista. Modeled on the staircase at the Villa d'Este on Lake Como, the steps will be lined with Japanese cedar, evoking the cypresses at the villa.

FILOLI

WOODSIDE, CALIFORNIA

Filoli was built in 1917 for William Bowers Bourn II, who owned a gold mine and a water company, two vital components of California life. Bourn chose his friend San Francisco architect Willis Polk to design the Georgian-style mansion. When the Bourns moved in, they hired Bruce Porter, a multitalented artist and garden designer, to create the sixteen-acre gardens. Porter made use of the splendid views to enhance his plan, which included parterres, lawns, a sunken garden, a yew allée, and greenhouses. It took ten years to complete.

Both the Bourns died in 1936, and Filoli was bought a year later by William and Lurline Roth, who understood the Bourn vision and enthusiastically took up the baton. The Roths were well placed to do this. Lurline was heir to the Matson Navigation Company, a successful shipping line operating out of San Francisco. When they married, William joined Matson, becoming general manager and vice president after the death of his father-in-law in 1916 and ultimately chairman of the board.

It was Lurline Roth who turned Filoli from a typical Gilded Age estate into an important horticultural destination. She became a dedicated gardener, studying every aspect of botany and climate. She collected rare plants, hunted for seeds, and eagerly propagated plants in her greenhouses. She also consulted Isabella Worn, known as Bella, who was a well-regarded designer in San Francisco and who had worked with Bruce Porter on the original design. Together they developed the gardens extensively, including the addition of a swimming pool and surrounding plantings.

Opposite: A Verona marble birdbath stands on the top tier of the Wedding Place amid a display of summer blooms.

Right: The pool in the sunken garden with the clock tower beyond.

The history of American gardens is filled with stories of profound relationships between clients and their garden designers. That between Roth and Worn was one of these. Worn went on to work for Julia Morgan at Hearst Castle in San Simeon and for other clients, but she never abandoned Filoli. A formidable figure, she worked right up until the day she died in 1950 at the age of eighty-one. Roth wrote after her death: "Filoli does not seem the same. Each and every plant reminds me of her . . . I will always think of her in this garden."

Above: The Georgian-style
garden house overlooks the
sunken garden.

Opposite: The knot garden
and herb garden with espal-
iered fruit trees and tall Irish
yews beyond.

By the 1970s, Roth was beginning to slow down, and her family convinced her to move. Filoli was quietly put up for sale, with the hope that a new owner might continue to maintain and keep the gardens open for the public. When the likely buyer announced the intention to turn the property into a horse farm, Roth balked. In 1975 she donated the house and gardens to the National Trust for Historic Preservation, along with an endowment that would maintain the property into the future. Under her guidance, in 1976 the nonprofit Filoli Center was created to manage the estate, and in 1978 the Friends of Filoli formed to bring together the volunteers and supporters who had already been working to protect the property. Roth continued to visit the gardens until her death in 1985, just after her ninety-fifth birthday.

Lurline Roth would be delighted to see her beloved Filoli today. The gardens continue to amaze; there is a trail system and nature hikes on the property; the Willis Polk house, with many pieces of original family furniture, is open; educational programs are presented year-round on horticulture, art, botany, and land preservation. Additions maintained by the Woodside-Atherton Garden Club and a perennial border donated by the Hillsborough Garden Club keep the gardens fresh for each new generation of visitors. A horse farm! One determined woman (and perhaps the ghost of her garden designer, Bella Worn) made sure Filoli had a very different future.

Left: Within the walled garden are beds of annuals enclosed by boxwood beneath a canopy of ginkgo trees.

Above: Ledges on the dining terrace display the bonsai collection.

Above: The mini knot garden is a gift of the Woodside-Atherton Garden Club.

Opposite: A hedge of hybrid yew surrounding the sunken garden is juxtaposed with Irish yews behind.

GREENWOOD GARDENS

SHORT HILLS, NEW JERSEY

The perspective is spectacular: high on a ridge toward the Watchung mountain range, with nothing but trees as far as the eye can see, although it is just forty-five minutes from Manhattan. The first house on the grounds was probably built in the late 1800s by Christian Feigenspan, a successful Newark brewer, but it burned down in 1911. Joseph P. Day, a wealthy real estate entrepreneur, replaced it with a twenty-eight-room mansion in the Arts and Crafts style, designed by architect William W. Renwick, whose more famous uncle James designed St. Patrick's Cathedral in New York. The gardens were planned in the same aesthetic, with colorful Rookwood glazed tile, a teahouse, a croquet lawn, a summer house, grottoes, pavilions, rustic stonework, and Asian statuary. This visual salad, combined with Italianate influences such as reflecting pools, fountains, classical columns, and interior metalwork by Samuel Yellin, the foremost ironmaster of the time, must have impressed even the most ambitious Gilded Age titans who were also building estates in New Jersey.

The Days' vast, impractical mansion was torn down in the 1950s and replaced with a more modest and traditional brick Colonial Revival house by its new owners, Peter P. Blanchard II and his wife, Adelaide, a granddaughter of Henry Clay Frick. They also favored a more traditional garden, replacing the extravagant flower borders with swaths of boxwood and yew, and adding grotesque statuary. The clash of eccentric meets traditional made for interesting gardening.

Opposite: The view from the cascade terrace, showing the formal allée of plane and maple trees created by Peter Blanchard III.

Right: The walls of the reflecting pool terrace are studded with Rookwood tiles, creating a colorful backdrop to the stone fountain.

Blanchard, a widower since 1956, died in 2000, by which time the garden had lost its way. However, he left instructions in his will that the property was to be preserved and passed on to an entity that could make it available for public enjoyment. His heirs, Peter P. Blanchard III and his wife, Sofia, accepted the responsibility for carrying out those wishes. They were encouraged by Frank Cabot, founder of the Garden Conservancy, who had visited the garden earlier and in 2001 brought in his experts to help the Blanchards make a plan. Walls, terraces, tilework, staircases, exedrae, pools, cascades, hedges, statuary, and colonnades all had to be reconstructed, and plantings recovered, working from old photographs and garden fabric remains. Public entrances and facilities had to be devised. Twenty-eight acres of exuberant garden design had to be recreated from the ruins. It was a huge undertaking and required help from many sources over the years.

Opposite: In the Garden of the Zodiac are remnants of a blue-tiled fountain with a bronze statue by Emilio Angela of a boy holding two geese.

Above: The house and steps leading to the croquet terrace, c. 1900.

Overleaf: The dramatic cascade, designed by William W. Renwick, with Rookwood tiles at the top, now awaiting restoration.

Once Greenwood Gardens had become a nonprofit organization, the New Jersey Historic Trust provided an initial funding grant and subsequently stepped in again with a matching grant, stimulating the Campaign for Greenwood Gardens. Historic Building Architects, led by Annabelle Radcliffe-Trenner, Rodney Robinson Landscape Architects, and local landscape architects and horticulturists joined forces to dig out, restore, and repair the infrastructure of the garden with all its idiosyncratic ornamentation. Louis Bauer was recruited from Wave Hill to help guide these efforts, which required the skills not only of builders, horticulturists, and gardeners, but tile experts, antiquarians, and archaeologists.

Phase 1, which included the restoration of the Sundial Terrace, retaining walls and main staircase, and all parking and entrances, is complete. Phase 2, which will focus on the waterworks, is in the planning stages. After immense efforts, the garden is now independent and was opened to the public in April 2013. "What is wonderful," Blanchard says, pointing to an archway with the stucco crumbling to reveal the brick beneath, "is that people seem to like the old atmosphere, the romance of it all, and the process."

Above: The staircase from the house to the reflecting pool has now been restored.

Opposite: This Fu dog is one of many Chinese elements in the gardens. The steps are now restored.

HISTORIC DEEPWOOD ESTATE
AND GAIETY HOLLOW

Elizabeth Lord and Edith Schryver are not as well known as their mentors Beatrix Farrand and Ellen Biddle Shipman, yet their contribution to the American landscape is just as noteworthy as that of their more famous colleagues. Lord and Schryver met in 1927 on a study tour of European gardens sponsored in part by the Lowthorpe School of Landscape Architecture in Groton, Massachusetts, where both women had studied at different times. They founded their design firm in 1929 in Salem, and the partnership was immediately successful. Lord was the plant expert, and Schryver the design and construction specialist. During their forty-year career, they created more than 250 designs in the Pacific Northwest.

In the history of American gardening, Lord and Schryver broke many boundaries. They were the first two women to jointly own a landscape firm in the region. They took on assignments that extended their range to institutional and civic projects. Their ideas about garden design diverged from the traditional approach of Gertrude Jekyll and Farrand. Lord and Schryver's look was described as "informal formality." Schryver said it best: "Too much neatness without careless grace will not produce charm." With a deep knowledge of horticulture, they introduced many new plants from the Northeast to their gardens on the West Coast and to the nurseries that sold them.

One of their important clients was Alice Bretherton Brown, the widow of the prominent Salem citizen Clifford Brown, who died in 1927. In 1924 the Browns bought from the Bingham family a large Victorian house designed by local architect William C. Knighton. After her husband's death, Alice Brown called in Lord and Schryver to develop the gardens, renaming the estate Deepwood. The designers created a series of garden rooms surrounding the house, including boxwood gardens and an English teahouse garden, along with arches, gazebos, glades, and flowerbeds glimpsed through ornamental gates.

In 1968 Alice, ill and frail, gave up the property, which remained unoccupied until the IBM corporation announced its intention to acquire it. Instead, a group of citizens purchased the

Opposite: The English teahouse garden at Deepwood, with loosely planted flowers framed by a rose-covered arch and gazebo.

Right and overleaf: Original wrought-iron fences give definition to the lower boxwood parterre.

Left and top: The lower
boxwood parterre today and
the original layout.

Above: Alice Bretherton
Brown, who commissioned the
boxwood parterre.

Opposite: Gaiety Hollow, Lord and Schryver's personal garden in Salem, before restoration.

Above left: Rhododendron walk and boxwood hedges.

Above right: Elizabeth Lord and Edith Schryver.

property and gave it to the city. In 1974 the Friends of Deepwood was founded to help the city manage the by now run-down estate. Deepwood Gardeners, another volunteer group, was formed specifically to work on the gardens.

A third nonprofit, the Lord & Schryver Conservancy, was founded in 2001 when locals became aware that the two great garden designers' legacy remained under threat. Today the park, known as Historic Deepwood Estate, is open to the public, and many social and community events take place there.

Another Lord & Schryver Conservancy project in Salem may ultimately take on even more significance. Perhaps the most important garden of the partnership was their own. For more than forty years they lived in the middle of Salem in a French country cottage–style house called Gaiety Hollow. Salem architect Clarence Smith, with whom they had collaborated on many projects, designed the house and garden in 1932 in the tradition of the great eighteenth-century English landscape architects such as Humphry Repton. While many of their commissions were for large urban properties, the two women relished the challenge of making a garden on less than an acre. In this minimal space, they could express their ideas about design and plant materials and show the world a perfect, and perfectly beautiful, blueprint of their artistic vision.

When Schryver died in 1984, the property sold to the Strand family. Sylvia Strand sold it to the Kingery family in 2013, and they are holding it for the Lord & Schryver Conservancy for five years. A capital campaign is underway to purchase the property, restore the wonderful little garden, and develop it into a sustainable financial entity. The Lord & Schryver Conservancy hopes to open the garden in 2015.

Opposite: A lush corner at Deepwood.

Above: Gaiety Hollow today, with paths, garden furniture, and fountains under restoration.

THE KAMPONG

MIAMI, FLORIDA

Kampong means "village" in Malay, and the garden was first planted with hundreds of species from Southeast Asia and other tropical regions by the legendary plant explorer Dr. David Fairchild. A botanical expert, Fairchild was hired by the U.S. Department of Agriculture to travel to the most remote parts of the world to find and import economically valuable plants, including soybeans, pistachios, mangoes, nectarines, dates, and cherries. In 1898 he started a garden for cultivating these tropical rarities in the climate most suitable for them: Miami, Florida.

In 1928 Fairchild and his wife, Marian, built a house and garden on Biscayne Bay in Coconut Grove, naming it The Kampong. It became one of the most exciting and important tropical gardens in the United States. People flocked to see the strange, otherworldly plants and trees that Fairchild had brought back from his many excursions, including new cultivars of avocado and mango, and hundreds of species of tropical fruit trees, flowering trees, and bamboo. David Fairchild died in 1954, though his name lives on in the garden named for him, the Fairchild Tropical Botanic Garden in Coral Gables. Marian stayed on at The Kampong until her death in 1962.

Opposite: Spring azaleas are juxtaposed with tropical foliage.

Right: An asoka tree, an endangered species originating in the rainforests of Asia and India.

At this point the garden might well have been in danger since the Fairchilds left no plans for its future nor any endowment. Fortunately, a year after Marian Fairchild's death, The Kampong was purchased by Edward and Catherine Sweeney, wealthy collectors, explorers, and world travelers. Catherine Sweeney, in particular, understood the importance of the Fairchilds' garden and assumed the daunting responsibility of taking care of the exotic, precious, and irreplaceable collections. In 1984 Dr. Sweeney donated The Kampong to the Pacific Tropical Botanical Garden (now the National Tropical Botanical Garden). That year she also negotiated for the garden to be placed on the National Register of Historic Places. She continued to live and work as patron and caretaker of the garden until her death in 1995.

By the time Dr. Sweeney died, her beloved Kampong had become a flourishing resource for students of botany and horticulture from all over the world. Succeeding

Above: A banyan tree, kept in check by a fiery red fence that reflects the colorful images of southeast Asia.

Right: The entrance to the house, a tamed jungle of tropical plants revealing a glimpse of Biscayne Bay.

directors have continued to ensure the maintenance and preservation of the collections, while fending off developers and other threats to their future. Today, The Kampong has become a major educational center, with dormitories, classrooms, and laboratory, under the aegis of the National Tropical Botanical Garden.

119

Opposite: Beside the pool are some of Fairchild's spectacular tropical finds, including a jacaranda tree.

Right: Purple Heart brightens the palette of greens.

THE GARDENS OF ALCATRAZ

SAN FRANCISCO, CALIFORNIA

The name Alcatraz does not immediately summon up an Eden of flowers, shrubs, sweet-smelling blooms. For most of us, Alcatraz remains the epitome of a brutal program of punishment and isolation from the world. But in one of the miracles of human endeavor, a series of extraordinary landscapes were created within these confines known for austerity and despair.

The island of Alcatraz was first settled in the mid-1800s, when its position in San Francisco Bay was recognized as a useful military outpost. In 1861 the barren landscape was turned into a military prison. Yet as early as 1865, local officials began importing soil from nearby islands and the mainland to start a garden near the summit. In the 1920s this effort was expanded with the support of the U.S. military and the California Spring Blossom and Wildflower Association, whose members organized prisoners to plant trees, shrubs, and seeds.

In 1933, when the Federal Bureau of Prisons took control of the island, the first warden's secretary, Fred Reichel, who was a keen horticulturist, decided to develop the gardens. Realizing he had a resident workforce, he recruited a group of maximum-security inmates to help. Soon some of the most dangerous criminals in the United States were digging, mulching, terracing, and planting the roughest terrain of the island, ultimately producing a dazzling array of blooming beds and borders.

Opposite: Only the shell of the original prison warden's house still stands. Low-maintenance plants now fill the garden.

Right: The decaying staircase leads down to the beach on the west side of the island, an area that has been left wild as a refuge for nesting birds.

"At first," Reichel wrote, "the authorities were fearful of allowing any 'resident' loose on the island, even though under the custody of a gun tower office." But soon most of them realized that it was more than a humane decision; it offered the hope that the prisoners might ultimately be restored to society. As ten-year inmate Elliott Michener wrote, "The hillside provided a refuge from disturbances of the prison, the work a release . . . This one thing I could do well."

Sadly, this productive and thoughtful program did not last. The federal prison closed in 1963, and in 1972 the island became part of the Golden Gate National Recreation Area. The gardens were abandoned, and without maintenance or water, the plants either died out or ran wild over the grounds. By the end of the twentieth century it was hard to believe that once upon a time this weed-infested island was covered in flowers.

Left: The foundations of the houses on "Officers' Row" are now garden plots. More than two hundred plants introduced to the island before 1963 still remain.

Right: One of the inmate gardeners surveying the "Officers' Row" garden plots in the 1940s.

Below: A greenhouse constructed by inmate gardener Elliott Michener, surrounded by the borders once so carefully maintained by the prisoners.

In 2003 the Garden Conservancy, the Golden Gate National Parks Conservancy, and the National Park Service joined together to rescue the gardens. With the help of grants, support from institutions such as the San Francisco Garden Club, the California Horticultural Society, and other public and private sources, plus consultation of archival photographs, memoirs, and other historical documents, the team was able to recreate five gardens, using the original plants cultivated by the earlier gardeners. They also added new plantings to supplement each area. A 330-foot trough that borders a main walkway toward the cell block is one of the most dramatic installations, completed in 2006. Old roses, fig trees, bulbs, and low-maintenance shrubs now flourish in this once-grim landscape, a welcoming sight for the 1.4 million visitors to the island each year.

Left: View from Alcatraz, looking east across the bay. In addition to original plants such as acanthus and chasmanthe, fifteen types of roses and other hardy plants have been added.

Above: Inmate gardens on the steep western slope are now partially restored, with the introduction of plants such as cosmos, nasturtiums, and gaillardias.

Opposite: Fruit trees planted by inmates survive on the west side of the island.

Right: Below the entrance to the cell block are the foundations of offices and residences, now transformed into gardens.

INNISFREE GARDEN

MILLBROOK, NEW YORK

Walter Beck, the builder of Innisfree, was born near Dayton, Ohio, in 1864. Beck's early interest in art was encouraged by a local art patron, who sent him to Germany to study. After a stint as a teacher at the Art Institute of Cincinnati, Beck moved to Pelham Manor, New York, where he quickly established himself in New York art circles. After the death of his first wife, he married Marion Burt Stone in 1922. Together they bought land in Millbrook and built a house they named Innisfree after the Yeats poem.

This land—now 185 acres of rolling hills, lakes, fields, and forests—became the overriding passion for the Becks. They began to study garden philosophy and garden art, inspired by the work of Asian artists, including the scroll paintings of the eighth-century Chinese poet, painter, and gardener Wang Wei they saw on display in the British Museum. Both Walter Beck's art and the garden plantings began to reflect these influences. At home he began developing a form of brush painting, and with his wife he started the creation of their life's work: the Chinese- and Japanese-style gardens of Innisfree.

Opposite: Stone Mountain in autumn. The central stone under the arch leads the eye back to the hillside.

Right: Hardy lotus and hydrangea paniculata surround the circular grotto. The rock forms suggest mythical Asian creatures.

In 1938 the Becks met Lester Collins, an encounter that was to turn into a lifelong friendship and collaboration for them all. At that time, Collins was still an undergraduate at Harvard, later graduating with a degree in English. After traveling in Asia with his friend landscape architect John O. Simons, Collins found his true calling, and in 1942 received a master's degree in landscape architecture at Harvard's Graduate School of Design. Collins went on to design many Eastern-influenced gardens and to acquire many distinguished clients including the Smithsonian in Washington, but his masterpiece was Innisfree, developed alongside the Becks for over fifty years. While shaping the wide-open landscape with rocks, shrubs, flowers, and developing the perimeter of a large, glacial lake, they dramatically changed the rhythms of the land into the form of what they called "cup gardens"— intimate, detailed garden rooms similar to but more random and unstructured than those Lawrence Johnston created at Hidcote in England. As Collins wrote in *Innisfree: An American Garden*: "Western gardens are usually designed to embrace a view of the whole . . .

Left: On the Middle Terrace the robust stonework is juxtaposed with columnar ginkgos and a bold blue spruce. The expansive lawn was originally a cutting garden.

Right: Owl Rock at the Point.

design revealed in a glance. The traditional Chinese garden is usually designed so that a view of the whole is impossible . . . The observer walks into a series of episodes, like Alice through the looking glass."

The Becks established the Innisfree Foundation, which they intended to endow for the "study of garden art at Innisfree," with resident scholars and educational programs. Sadly, the expenses of Marion Beck's last illness depleted the funds, and the garden was left unsupported. There were suggestions that the property should be sold, but supporters of the garden instead sold off artwork from the Becks' collections, eliminated staff and gardeners, and removed fragile plantings. Thanks to these and other efforts, the garden remained afloat and was opened to the public in 1960.

Collins, who never gave up even during the dark days, continued to expand and refine the various garden areas, simplifying some for economic reasons, enhancing some after storms or when microclimates changed, always finding new ways to express the inexpressible. His immersion in Innisfree and its magical environment continued until his death in 1993. In the early 1970s, part of the land surrounding the original acreage was sold to Rockefeller University, thus shoring up the endowment. Today, the Innisfree Foundation runs the garden and public programs independently of any other institution.

Above: The Middle Terrace looking north to Tiptoe Rock.

Opposite: The lakeshore by the Meadow. Innisfree chairs, designed by Lester Collins were influenced by the work of Rietveld.

Left: The fountain jet seen from Dumpling Knoll.

Opposite: The vista to the Point, with Turtle, Dragon, and Owl Rocks, and on through the channel to Stone Mountain.

ANNE SPENCER GARDEN

LYNCHBURG, VIRGINIA

A poet, a civil rights activist, a teacher, and a gardener, Anne Bethel Scales Bannister Spencer was an important figure of the Harlem Renaissance. She helped found the Lynchburg Chapter of the NAACP and worked tirelessly for the cause from the 1920s onward. Her husband, Edward, a postman, storeowner, and landlord, helped build the extraordinary garden where she spent much of her time, creating brightly painted pergolas, birdhouses, a formal garden with a pond, and masses of flowers. Interestingly, her poetry was less about race—a topic favored by most African-American writers of her time—and more about nature. Her biographer J. Lee Greene remarked on her poetic kinship with Emily Dickinson, Walt Whitman, and Robert Browning. It is clear, then, that her garden was a crucial part of her creativity and inspiration.

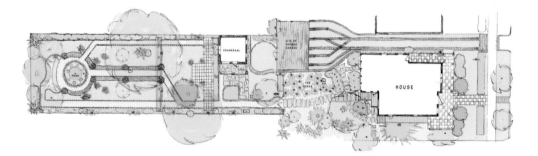

Opposite: Pink roses contrast brightly with the blue-painted pavilion, now restored to its original color.

When Anne Spencer died in 1975, family members and the community worked together to keep her legacy alive, and the property became a Virginia Historic Landmark in 1977. The house required the maintenance and restoration typical of all old houses, particularly for such individual and colorful decoration. The overgrown, neglected garden was another matter entirely, and here a local garden club took charge. The Hillside Garden Club adopted the garden in 1983 and immediately set to work, with the help of archival photographs and local memoirists, to reclaim the framework and as much original planting as possible, including Spencer's own bulbs and roses. In 1987 this restoration received the Common Wealth Award from the Garden Club of Virginia.

By 2007 the infrastructure was struggling again. This time members of the Hillside Garden Club, with the encouragement of the Garden Conservancy, rebuilt the pergola, arbor, and for the first time restored the pond. The wooden structures are now painted in the same bright robins' egg blue that Spencer had selected. Photographs taken over the years confirm that the garden has been restored almost exactly to its original splendor (garnering a second Common Wealth Award) in a wonderful tribute to the vivid personalities of Anne and Edward Spencer, who first designed it.

Left: Anne and Edward Spencer with two of their grandchildren, 1930s.

Below: The Spencers seated by the pond, 1937.

Opposite: A lily pond terminates the walkway from the house through the garden.

Above: Clusters of peonies surround the elegantly carved pillars supporting the pavilion.

Right: The cottage is called "Edankraal," an African word meaning dwelling or enclosure.

LADEW TOPIARY GARDENS

MONKTON, MARYLAND

Harvey Smith Ladew was one of those wonderful bachelor characters who might have sprung from the mind of P. G. Wodehouse. In his early years Ladew, the only son of a leather manufacturer, decided to dedicate the first fifty years of his life to enjoyment. Work, he reckoned, could come later. Actually, he had been preparing for this career since birth, his education consisting mostly of dancing lessons, riding to hounds, and world traveling. "I could order breakfast in five languages," he later recalled.

In 1929 he bought and rebuilt Pleasant Valley Farm, in Baltimore horse country. The property consisted of a house dating from the mid-eighteenth century and 250 acres of land. With the help of decorators Billy Baldwin and Ruby Ross Wood, Ladew transformed the interiors with a splendid collection of European antiques and fine furniture, mostly purchased abroad by Ladew himself, and the house became a vivid expression of his refined and eclectic eye.

While the house was full of charm, it was the garden that expressed the fullest extent of his personality. While foxhunting in England, Ladew saw a very realistic topiary foxhunt carved out of a hedge. He immediately decided to try to reproduce this wonderful "living sculpture" back home in Baltimore. Using a mixture of yew and hemlock, he soon created not only the foxhunt, but also swans, dogs, lyrebirds, and all sorts of abstract circles and obelisks. Visitors—some of them famous, such as Moss Hart, Edna Ferber, and Cole Porter—were astonished and delighted since topiary was not yet an art form in the United States. Inspired by visits to gardens in England, Ladew also created fifteen garden rooms, each leading into the other in strict succession. He ordered up from his fertile imagination a Tivoli Tea House, a Temple of Venus, and a huge lawn amphitheater, the Great Bowl, encircled by high hemlock hedges with a fountain at its center.

Opposite: Green hounds cross the lawn in Ladew's quirky vision of a topiary garden.

Right: A top-hatted gentleman on horseback takes the garden gate in stride.

The gardens were opened to the public on a limited basis in 1968, and Ladew founded with friends a private nonprofit foundation, Ladew Topiary Gardens, Inc., to maintain the house and gardens and raise funds for its financial sustainability. Harvey Ladew died in 1976 after a long illness, and the young foundation directed its efforts toward the declining gardens and upkeep of the house. Thoughtful management policies and the concerted effort of local

Above: Topiary, pools,
fountains, and clipped hedges
enliven the landscape.

Opposite: Animals rise up
mysteriously from the banks of
grasses that line the perimeter
of the garden.

Overleaf: The central bowl of
the garden seems to glow in
the magical dawn light.

supporters and friends helped the foundation restore and better prepare the property for the public. Today the house and gardens (the historic core of which consists of twenty-two acres) are on the National Register of Historic Places, and the Ladew Topiary Gardens foundation continues to raise funds in multiple ways to ensure that Ladew's wild, witty, and original vision may be enjoyed for generations to come.

YEW DELL BOTANICAL GARDENS

CRESTWOOD, KENTUCKY

Arborist, farmer, horticulturist, plant collector, teacher, visionary—all these terms describe Theodore Klein, who, with his wife, Martha Lee, developed the thirty-three-acre property not far from Louisville, Kentucky that is now the Yew Dell Botanical Gardens, famous for its thousands of specimen trees, plant nursery, display gardens, and a genuine castle.

Klein came from a long line of farmers who made their homes in Kentucky. They raised flowers and plants for commercial distribution, planted trees, and owned horses, cows, hogs, sheep, and chickens. But Klein had more specific ambitions. He became interested in hollies and began to collect them, planting them in the fields he acquired over the years from family and neighbors. Self-taught, he traveled to nurseries across the country and abroad, studying not only hollies but also many other species of trees and plants that he would bring home to experiment on. He was a brilliant grafter, and he kept meticulous records of his work. Dorothy Lammlein, author of the Klein family history, quotes from his records: "Grafted corotys, pink viburnum tomentosa, worked on Camden Acres House and Castle. Grafted Thompson Blue Spruce . . . Grafted beech from A (Arnold?) Arboretum."

Opposite: The sunken rock garden was one of the first created by Theodore Klein. Built of local Louisville limestone, it is now used as a test garden for alpine and tropical succulents.

Right: The arboretum.

Theodore Klein became famous for his nursery at Yew Dell and for his exceptional knowledge of historic trees and plants. People consulted him from all over, and he generously gave away cuttings to almost anyone who asked for them. He built a modest Cotswolds-style stone house for his family, which stands beside an astonishing piece of architecture that could only have come from an unconventional mind. It is a gray stone castle, with turrets, a porch, and steeply pitched roof. He and Martha Lee lived out their lives at Yew Dell with four children, all of whom stayed close to home. At his death in 1998, Klein had introduced more than sixty new plants into the United States, as well as nurturing more than a thousand rare trees and shrubs and creating a series of dazzling formal gardens. He was buried next to his wife in the Floydsburg Cemetery, in a piece of ground that had been part of Martha Lee's family farm. *Courier-Journal* columnist Bob

Left: An original barn was restored as an event and program space with a new pavilion adjacent.

Opposite: A peony border runs alongside the secret garden, which is planted with hellebores, ferns, and hostas.

Hill wrote of this serene plot: "Above them both like an umbrella from God—are the spreading limbs of a beautiful black gum tree."

With his death, potential development began to threaten the arboretum, which, curiously, was zoned for commercial use. Local volunteers and other supporters raised the funds to purchase Yew Dell from the Klein family in 2002 and started the long and arduous process of restoring it and organizing it as a sustainable public space. The Garden Conservancy played a significant role in this process, naming it a Preservation Project and generating a stabilization plan that would help local forces structure the rehabilitation of the gardens, grounds, and buildings. Today, Yew Dell is a nationally recognized treasure trove of unusual trees and plants, along with a research center, buildings, and display gardens that attract visitors from all over the world.

Above: A holly allée borders
the sunken garden.

Right: The sunken rock
garden.

154

Left: A purple European beech, now known as 'Klein Copper.'

Opposite: A weeping Norway spruce in the arboretum, a ten-acre area where Klein carried out long-term testing of trees.

LOTUSLAND

SANTA BARBARA, CALIFORNIA

One of the more exotic gardens in the United States, Lotusland was created by a wildly unconventional Polish woman, who became Ganna Walska, a multiply married opera singer, supporter of Tibetan monks, socialite, and ultimately garden designer.

Walska's operatic pursuits did not live up to expectations, although an opera house was named after her. Although her singing failed to launch her to stardom, she continued to study music throughout her life. For solace, she turned to spiritual matters, and her life became a continual search for enlightenment, both in North America and Europe. She tried marriage six times, and finally, at the urging of her last husband, Theos Bernard, purchased the thirty-seven-acre Cuesta Linda estate in Santa Barbara in 1941.

The idea was to turn the property into a retreat for Tibetan monks, and it was originally named Tibetland. But when wartime restrictions prevented the monks from traveling, she renamed the property Lotusland after the Indian lotus plant and turned her attention to her garden. Immersing herself in the study of rare plants, in particular succulents, she used her vivid imagination to create a serious botanical display garden, with ferns, palms, aloes, bromeliads, cacti, and other strange growing things. Lockwood de Forest and Ralph Stephens were two of the several landscape designers who helped her develop this hallucinatory landscape, adding unusual plants and laying out pools and paths ornamented with shells and Moorish tiles. There is an almost Disneyland feel to the place, with an Elizabethan amphitheater, topiary, jungly woodland, and an abalone-lined pond punctuated by three-tiered shell fountains. Surrounding the pink stucco house, hundreds of spectacular cacti thrust upward like the weapons of armed guards protecting their flamboyant owner.

Opposite: The lotus pond, filled with the lovely eponymous flowers, rises up before an allée of cypress trees.

Right: Between 1968 and 1972, one of the ponds was converted into a Japanese-style garden.

Walska continued working on her garden until the end of her life, selling her jewelry if necessary to obtain some unattainable botanical treasure. "Usually the emotional capacity of the feelings diminished with age but my powers of feeling have remained unrestrained," she wrote modestly in her autobiography. She died in 1984 at the age of ninety-seven. Attentive to the last, she left her estate to the nonprofit Ganna Walska

Left: A huge sea-clam fountain feeds water into the abalone-shell pool.

Above: Some of Ganna Walska's amazing collection of agaves, cacti, and other succulents.

Lotusland Foundation, which maintains the property, opening it to the public on a strictly regulated basis and presenting programs for educational purposes. Lotusland is a creation as passionate and melodramatic as any of the grand operas this Polish diva failed to conquer. Walska's garden is her ultimate triumph; her performance here will never be forgotten.

Above and opposite: Massive spears of cacti and agaves rise up like guardians to protect the garden.

Overleaf: A winding path leads through spectacular topiary toward the massed tropical collections arrayed under the trees.

GARLAND FARM

BAR HARBOR, MAINE

Beatrix Farrand, the most famous landscape gardener of her day, designed some of the finest gardens in America, including Dumbarton Oaks in Washington, D.C., the Abby Aldrich Rockefeller Garden in Seal Harbor, Maine, and parts of the Princeton and Yale University campuses. Yet her last garden—the one she perhaps treasured the most—was nearly lost to us forever.

Beatrix Farrand spent most of her summers with her husband, Max, at Reef Point, their large family home and world-famous garden in Bar Harbor, Maine. Around 1939 the Farrands incorporated the Reef Point Gardens in the state of Maine. After her husband's death in 1945, Farrand found the property increasingly difficult to run. The postwar mood was not hospitable to providing the kind of maintenance such estates required, costs mounted prodigiously, and there was little or no public support. Rather than watch the property decline, she decided to have the house torn down and the garden (including the plants) dismantled. The University of California at Berkeley received her books and herbarium specimens, and many plants were acquired by local designer Charles Savage, who found homes for them in the Thuya and Asticou Azalea Gardens in Northeast Harbor, Maine.

Opposite: The wooden wall of the Terrace Garden was once a cornice. It was salvaged from the house of one of Farrand's clients and recycled at Reef Point.

Right: A window overlooking the Terrace Garden.

Reef Point ceased to exist in 1955, and Farrand retired to Garland Farm, a cottage not far from Bar Harbor that belonged to her chauffeur and handyman, Lewis Garland, and his wife, Amy. Garland had been the principal caretaker at Reef Point, and his wife the chief gardener and horticulturalist. After adding a wing to the house, Farrand moved in with her companion, Clementine Walter. In this modest setting she began her final garden, pouring her talent, imagination, and horticultural knowledge into the small patch of ground surrounding the house. It is said that she brought her favorite plants with her to Garland Farm.

Beatrix Farrand died at Garland Farm in 1959 at the age of eighty-seven. The Garlands and two subsequent owners lived on in the house, with the garden mostly forgotten, until 1998, when landscape architect Patrick Chassé received some very startling news. Chassé had just

Above: French doors from Clementine Walter's sitting room open on to the garden. Farrand planted this area with the brightly colored blooms her companion preferred.

Opposite: Farrand's sitting room overlooked this part of the garden, which she planted with her favorite palette of grays, blues, and yellows. The fences came from Reef Point.

given a lecture on Farrand in Bar Harbor, when an elderly woman, Virginia Eveland, went up to him and told him that she lived at Garland Farm, and that traces of Farrand's garden were still there. Chassé was astonished. He had thought it long gone.

But gardens, if given the chance, have a tendency to survive. When Chassé visited Garland Farm, he found the gardens still intact, though mostly buried under what he called "woolly remains." In 2003 Jim and Edith Fuchs founded the Beatrix Farrand Society, with Chassé as first president, with the express purpose of restoring and preserving the Garland Farm garden and creating a Beatrix Farrand archive, research library, and educational center on the property.

The Garland Farm revival is probably one of the most complex and well-documented garden rescues in America. In 2005 the Beatrix Farrand Society commissioned a cultural landscape report from Pressley Associates. The following year the University of Maine Master Gardener Volunteers Advisory Council voted to select the Garland Farm Terrace Restoration as a volunteer project, under Master Gardener Carolyn Hollenbeck. The Terrace Garden is at the back of the house. It was designed in the form of a 40-by-44-foot parterre, with nine rectangular raised beds (a Farrand signature), framed with roof tiles and bordered by a fence and paneling, all from Reef Point. After so long, much of the material was unrecognizable.

The Terrace Garden transformation began in 2007. Heather beds and stepping-stones were cleaned out. Plants were removed and placed in a holding garden, each numbered and marked for repositioning. Perennials were sorted as original or anachronous. Bulbs were

dug up, soil collected for analysis, buried tiles recovered. The volunteer team consulted contemporary books, catalogs, and most important, an article about the garden published in 1962, just three years after Farrand's death, by Mary Alice Roche, which included a picture of the planting plan. "This was our Rosetta Stone," Hollenbeck said.

By the end of 2012, the planting was complete. In the end, ninety-five different types of plants were brought back to the garden. Perhaps the most exciting moments came with the rediscovery of an Asian statue and a cistern that were visible in early photographs. It turned out that in 1964 Amy Garland had given the statue to David Rockefeller's wife, Peggy, for the Abby Aldrich Rockefeller Garden, which is replete with Asian motifs. The cistern was purchased in the mid-1960s by Charles Savage and was on display in the Thuya Garden in Northeast Harbor. Both the statue and the cistern have returned to Garland Farm.

In a strange twist of fate, Beatrix Farrand had left a codicil in her will that the Garland Farm garden was to be demolished if she outlived the Garlands and they found no suitable purchasers. As with Reef Point, she could not bear to contemplate the desecration, through ignorance or neglect, of her last and most precious creation. How fortunate that her heirs at Garland Farm and a group of committed admirers heard Farrand's voice and gave her final and most personal garden its deserved place in the sun for years to come.

Above: There were ninety-nine plants on the original plant list, including lavender, campanula, dianthus, nepeta, aquilegia, iris, delphinium, artemisia, and roses.

Opposite left: An Asian statue, once considered lost forever, is now back in place.

Opposite right: The birdbath is a copy of one seen in an early photograph.

171

MADOO GARDEN

SAGAPONACK, NEW YORK

Friends have fond memories of Robert Dash in a long overcoat striding down the garden path at Madoo waving a glass of champagne and calling, "Welcome!" Few gardens could live up to such a greeting, but his never failed. Dash was a painter before he was a gardener. Born in New York City, he was interested in poetry, music, and painting from an early age. Working as an editor in New York after college, he met the poets James Schuyler, John Ashbery, and Frank O'Hara, among other artists. But painting soon became his principal interest. Self-taught, he like to work both from nature and in abstract forms. He had his first solo show in 1961, and his art is now in both institutional and private collections.

Dash purchased the Sagaponack property in 1967 and started designing the garden around an old barn dating from 1740, which served as his studio and summer living quarters. Gardening seemed to strike a chord in him, combining as it did so many of his passions—nature, art, poetry, music, the life of the mind. Dash was an intimidating man. He could be difficult, impatient with stupidity, intolerant of hypocrisy, and mercurial with strangers. But in the garden, he found his ease and contentment.

The plot is tiny—under two acres—but it feels much larger, thanks to the brilliant landscaping of the artist. He envisioned a series of small rooms that included an Asian water garden, a potager, and a parterre garden, connected with bridges and an intricate pattern of pathways. At the far end, the garden opens up to reveal the flat expanse of potato fields so typical of eastern Long Island.

Since he was a painter, visual morsels are scattered provocatively in this small space. For instance, a shady pathway is shocked into brightness by a garden gate painted lime-green—a color he changed on a whim every year (currently bright blue). A woodshed with mirrored panels reflects light and subtle angles of the garden. He built a pergola, shamelessly copying his good friend Rosemary Verey's laburnum walk at Barnsley House in England. Inside the barn, the visitor experiences different views of the garden, each framed by the windows like a painting.

Opposite: Brightly colored paint is a hallmark of this artist's garden. Here blue and green steps lead to a rooftop overlook.

Right: This garden is filled with whimsical detail, such as this garden fence and its dried plant decoration.

Left: Robert Dash used all sorts of garden furniture for his designs, such as this urn with a metal frame for a plant to climb up when it feels like it.

Opposite: A blue gazebo stands in the dappled shade. In front is a dwarf weeping willow tree planted between two boxwoods.

Overleaf: Plane trees serve as a canopy for this seating area, with a reflecting pool and mixed border beyond.

Over the years, more and more people begged to see Dash's masterpiece, and as he grew older, it was clear that a plan for its preservation was in order. In 1993 he deeded the property to the Madoo Conservancy, retaining life tenancy. The conservancy's role is to study and preserve the unique designs, features, and plantings that he created with such artistry. Dash believed that a garden is like a spiritual biography. "So making a garden," he explained, "means knowing who you are." Thanks to his talent, generosity, and foresight, those who never met him will know, through his garden, something of who he was.

PECKERWOOD GARDEN

HEMPSTEAD, TEXAS

The history of this garden began in 1971, when John G. Fairey, a teacher in the school of architecture at Texas A&M University, acquired the land that became Peckerwood, his monument to the various plants he brought over the years from Mexico, Asia, and all across the United States to thrive in the challenging Texas landscape. The land he purchased, fifty minutes west of downtown Houston and now almost forty acres, is a repository for more than 3,000 rare and unusual plants, including drought-tolerant and threatened species, that make up the core Peckerwood collection.

Fairey is a pioneer in horticulture, plant research, and cultivation, deeply committed to spreading the word about plants and their habitats. Over the years he has organized expeditions to collect seeds and plants from Mexico and other countries, and various institutions in the United States, Great Britain, and Korea are now involved in the exchange of seeds and plant materials.

The garden is an astonishing sight, a naturalistic landscape that brings together some of the most exotic and rare trees and plants ranging from Asia to South America. Fairey applied his background as a painter to develop the garden as a series of ravishing canvases of texture and color as well as a laboratory for scientific education. "It is a garden with a mission to encourage other gardeners to see a beauty in landscape that is consistent with our plants and climate," he says. "It is a pioneering garden exploring new plants and cultivation methods for other gardeners. It is a garden that looks to the future, not to the past."

Opposite: Red Yucca flower and an Agave americana.

Right: Agave ovatifolia from Mexico and Nolina nestonii with a Peacock Flower.

In 1986 Fairey founded the Yucca Do Nursery with Carl Schoenfeld, selling plants and seeds from the garden, with the profits going toward maintenance. But as the garden grew, so did the expenses. Plans were made to turn Peckerwood into a public garden, and to that end the Garden Conservancy named Peckerwood as a preservation project garden in 1998. The same year the Peckerwood Garden Conservation Foundation was established to help maintain and operate the garden. With these groups working to develop it as an educational and research center as well as a source of continuing aesthetic pleasure, it opened to the public for the first time in 2014. In pioneer John Fairey's prescient words, "In this world of overemphasized technology in which values are often based on the superficial, gardens are a must for the public."

Adove: In the beds in front of a
blue wall inspired by Frida
Kahlo's garden are Beaked
Yucca and Spanish Dagger
with Walter's Viburnum in the
foreground

Opposite: Saw Palmetto lines
the path to a pergola with
Walter's Viburnum beyond.

Above: The pool and fountain wall in the courtyard were instpired by the work of Luis Barragan. The sculpture on the gate is by Texas artist Lars Stanley.

PEARL FRYAR TOPIARY GARDEN

BISHOPVILLE, SOUTH CAROLINA

One day in the early 1980s, Pearl Fryar came upon a neatly clipped shrub in a nursery, and it changed his life. Fryar was a modest but untrained gardener, and the sight of this shapely green ball transformed him almost overnight into an obsessive student of topiary, who ultimately created an astonishing three-acre topiary garden on his property in Bishopsville.

Self-taught and with inexhaustible energy, he gradually built a landscape, mostly employing junipers, hollies, cypress, pines, and oaks, shaped to perfection with a hedge trimmer. His abstract designs look like animals, fans, three-tiered cakes, circles, diamonds, triangles, pom-poms—nothing is beyond Fryar's artistic ambition. "I like to let people see what they want to in my plants," he told the *Lee County Observer* in 1993. "The creativity comes in making a shape that speaks to me in one way but may say something else to everyone else." While the five hundred topiary shapes he has designed dazzle visitors from all over the world, Fryar's garden also spreads the inspiring message that a single individual, self-taught and with admirable determination, can create a place that expresses, in his words, "Love, Peace, and Goodwill."

Opposite: A sculpture garden of topiary nestles in front of its suburban neighbors, one of the original trimmed pine trees soaring above.

Right: In the newer part of the garden, enormous, fanciful topiary shapes rise into the sky.

Overleaf: An abundant display of plants not always used in topiary, including cypress and oaks.

But as the garden grew, so did the maintenance effort. Keeping a topiary garden in shape, literally, is a major task, and impossible for one person to manage alone. As Fryar and the garden grew older, the work became more and more challenging. In 2006 the Pearl Fryar Topiary Garden Inc. was formed in partnership with the Garden Conservancy to maintain and preserve his work for generations to come. Thanks to these organizations, Fryar's magnificent obsession will continue to inspire and give pleasure as long as his uniquely personal garden exists.

Above: The artist chooses
not to represent animals—
the most common form of
topiary—preferring abstract
shapes that spring from his
imagination.

Opposite: Pearl Fryer's modest
house belies the complexity
of the topiary world that
surrounds it.

HOLLISTER HOUSE GARDEN

WASHINGTON, CONNECTICUT

Tucked away in the northwestern corner of Connecticut is a garden that is, to borrow a phrase from the English poet Rupert Brooke, "forever England." The garden unfolds in a series of "rooms," with blowsy perennial borders, stretches of lawn, a walled garden, apple trees, a parterre, a winding stream, and a vegetable garden. This timeless landscape is largely the creation of George Schoellkopf, who is quick to acknowledge his debt to the input of various friends and informal advisors. He started planning it in 1979, and since then, it has become one of the most highly regarded gardens in the United States.

Schoellkopf was born in 1942 in Dallas, Texas, where even as a child he was attempting to make gardens. He owned a gallery of eighteenth- and nineteenth-century American antiques in New York for many years, honing his eye, but allowing for only weekend gardening. It wasn't until 1979 that he was able to give his full attention to the garden at Hollister House. He had become an experienced horticulturist, and the garden grew exponentially from then on.

Schoellkopf's inspiration is evident. He studied Hidcote, Sissinghurst, and Great Dixter, three of England's preeminent gardens, and translated them into an American idiom. Thus the "rooms," the choice of plant materials, and the color palettes will remind any English garden-lover of his muses across the pond. But he has also added his own personal contributions: a sunken terrace, plants such as the primulas developed by his Vermont colleagues Joe Eck and Wayne Winterrowd, and new vistas across the property.

Opposite: A path from the house leads down into the walled garden.

Right: A massive glazed urn at the head of the reflecting pool.

In 2005 Schoellkopf made the important gesture this garden deserved: he formed an independent nonprofit corporation, in partnership with the Garden Conservancy, called Hollister House Garden Inc., to which he is gradually donating the entire property, including his house and various outbuildings. During his lifetime, while retaining a tenancy, he has promised to be solely responsible for the maintenance and operation of the property, as well as creating a sizable endowment to support it after his death. Since this unprecedented gift, Hollister House Garden has been visited by thousands, and a continuing effort at educational outreach has resulted in annual Garden Study Weekends,

Above: and opposite: Trimmed
boxwood encloses the beds in
the formal garden.

Overleaf: The reflecting pool
in late spring.

attended by a sell-out number of garden aficionados. The garden is now listed on the National Register of Historic Places, a well-deserved honorific for one of the most brilliant gardens in the United States and one that, thanks the generosity of Schoellkopf, will continue in perpetuity.

MONTROSE

HILLSBOROUGH, NORTH CAROLINA

"It was the beginning of the greatest adventure of my life." This was how Nancy Goodwin described the purchase, with her husband, Craufurd, of Montrose in 1977. The late-nineteenth-century house sits on sixty-one acres of picturesque open space, originally landscaped by William Alexander Graham and his wife, Susan, with the help of Thomas Paxton, garden designer for the University of North Carolina at Chapel Hill.

The Goodwins' original idea was simply to maintain and extend the original plantings. But its potential turned Nancy, who taught music for a profession, into an avid gardener. Within a few years, she had become acquainted with thousands of plants, flowers, and shrubs that would grow in the rich Hillsborough clay loam—perennials, vegetable gardens, bulbs, and extraordinary trees such as the two metasequoias that tower eighty feet above her front lawn. She became a gardener's gardener—an encyclopedia of rare, native, or underutilized flowers, such as hardy cyclamen, winter jasmine, Formosa lilies, and a coral bell that is now named "Montrose Ruby," after its propagator.

Nancy Goodwin talks about her garden like a painter. She focuses on color—waves of it—and pattern— paths that wind through the rich landscape—and light and shade. She studies the seasons like a meteorologist, planning the flowering times so that the garden is blooming year-round. She is also a prolific writer. A chronicle of a year in her gardens entitled *Montrose: Life in a Garden* as well as many articles for *Horticulture* and other magazines have disseminated her philosophy and knowledge to readers all over the world.

Opposite: In early spring, drifts of hellebore and phlox divaricata give a soft Southern feel to the garden.

Right: An elaborately framed arbor serves as an entrance to the garden.

Goodwin is now seventy-nine years old. Some years ago, in discussion with her husband, she decided Montrose should be put on firm financial footing for the future. In 2001, Montrose was placed on the National Register of Historic Places. The Goodwins established a conservation easement on fifty acres of the property, in association with the Triangle Land Conservancy. They have also set up a separate entity, the Montrose Foundation, Inc., which will be the beneficiary of the house and the gardens after their deaths. This is the magnificent gift that Nancy Goodwin is leaving to the world: her unique passion, knowledge, and horticultural genius.

Above and opposite: Greens
and blues are the dominant
colors, with iris and euphorbia
mingling beautifully together.

Opposite: A black-painted urn is surrounded by the subtle colors of euphorbia, one of Nancy Goodwin's favorites.

Above: Drifts of phlox, alchemilla, and kniphofia form the spring floor of the woodland garden.

CHARLES RICHARDS GARDEN

GREAT WASS ISLAND, MAINE

This garden is in the farthest reaches of southeastern Maine, on a point overlooking the Gulf of Maine. On clear days it offers a view of Cadillac Mountain on Mount Desert Island. Here, on a granite ledge, Charles Richards, emeritus professor of botany at the University of Maine in Orono, decided to create a garden.

It took him roughly thirty years. He used the site—nearly three acres and a small cottage— as a vacation place during his tenure at Orono. For almost twenty years, the professor and his students would go there, enjoying the ocean views, the rocky landscape, and a small boat. In 1982, when Richards retired, he decided he wanted a garden. From that moment on, he took the most intransigent topography—bare, windswept, lacking the most rudimentary soil—and transformed it, inch by inch, into a magical landscape of trees, flowers, stone paths, and undulating carpets of moss.

"I never had a plan," he says. "I just started, doing it in pieces, creeping further and further away from the house each year. I planted most of the trees. I brought soil in. I did a lot of experiments. I found pockets in the rock where I could plant flowers. Every year different things happened." The work was backbreaking. He had to strip the enormous granite ledges of their tenacious layers of sheep laurel and chokeberry. He had to plant more than one hundred trees, mostly spruce and fir. He had to bring in rocks and plants by boat—as well as countless tons of topsoil. Gradually he began to see results. Astilbes, hostas, primulas, astrantias, potentillas, callunas, and numerous ferns flourished under his persuasive and patient hands. Rare plants such as astilboides and rodgersia also found their way into the midst of his native collections.

Perhaps the most striking aspect of the garden is the moss, which after all these years of nurturing, rolls over the rock formations like soft green fabric, leaving spongy pools along the paths, and creating strange fairy-tale shapes in the shadows between the high profiles of the trees.

Richards is now ninety-four years old. He cannot do the planting or weeding he once did and finds it difficult to train young people to distinguish between a flower and a weed. He does not stake. He waters using a handheld hose. He put up a fence to stop the deer from their inexorable progress, but there are signs his barrier is not impregnable. Visitors and friends still come from all over, awed by the beauty and originality of what he has made. But his

Opposite: In the wooded areas of the property, Charles Richards encouraged the local moss to thrive.

Right: Hostas and ferns are favorite ground-cover plants that give subtle color to the landscape.

Above and right: The contrast between the unforgiving rock and the flourishing plant material testifies to the effort of creating this garden.

Overleaf: At times it is impossible to believe that this display of rhododendrons, spirea, foxgloves, mixed shrubs, and evergeens was raised from massive slabs of Maine granite.

family is not interested in taking responsibility for its future. Local and state organizations are unable to take on such a challenge, particularly since the problem of parking is insoluble. Part of Great Wass Island is a nature reserve. Couldn't this treasure of a garden be annexed in some way? At this point there are no answers. The gardener himself is philosophical. "It will go back to Nature," he says. After all it was only borrowed from Nature in the first place.

Left: A soft green carpet of moss unrolls over the decaying trees, once planted by Richards, and now left lying where they fall.

A LIFE IN THE GARDEN

CURTICE TAYLOR

Like so many fulfilling obsessions, *Rescuing Eden* comes out of events of long ago. The project owes its genesis to three icons of design and style: Russell Page, the preeminent English garden designer, William S. Paley, the formidable chairman of CBS, and his wife, Babe Paley, beautiful and vivacious doyenne of New York society.

My father, Frank Taylor, a publisher, had met Russell Page in London after the war, and the two became close friends. I met Russell for the first time in 1970 when he came for lunch at our house in Connecticut, which was not far from the garden he was working on for Mary Lasker. He was very tall—well over six feet—with a large face and bald head, Oxbridge accent, formidable yet charming, and conversant with any cultural subject. A few years later when I was studying and teaching at SUNY Purchase, I visited him while he was creating the remarkable gardens at the Pepsico headquarters across the road from the campus. I was just beginning to embrace photography but never lifted a camera in a garden.

In 1979 I received a call from a distressed Page. "The English photographer hired by *Country Life* has gone off on a bender," he explained. "You are the only photographer I know in New York. Do you think you can photograph Bill and Babe Paley's garden for the magazine?" I replied, "I can certainly try, but you have to be there to show me how." Without exaggeration, thus began my career as a garden photographer.

The Paleys' driver picked me up at 5:30 AM and drove me to Kiluna Farm, their estate on Long Island where Page met me. He taught me the first rule of garden photography: shoot only early in the morning or the late afternoon. "Do not use a wide angle lens, though you may be tempted, because it distorts the landscape and throws off the design" was another invaluable bit of advice.

The garden was magnificent and in full spring bloom, but the house seemed abandoned. I learned that Mrs. Paley had recently died of cancer and that Russell and Mr. Paley had been constantly at her bedside. In addition to overseeing the photography of the garden for Country Life, Russell was designing a series of hedges to surround her grave. Mr. Paley had moved to another house in Southampton where Russell was designing a new garden. The fate of the Kiluna Farm garden troubled Russell: "So many of my gardens have gone and this is my best American effort."

The *Country Life* article was published with five of my photographs in March 1980, launching my career. Shortly thereafter Mr. Paley asked to see the rest of the images, and I brought them to his office at "Black Rock," the CBS headquarters in Midtown.

After seeing them, he surprised me by asking, "Can you go back and photograph the entire place, the buildings and the landscape?" I went back four times and assembled a record of the remarkable estate. Later in the summer, when I presented the photographs to him, he was so deeply moved that I realized that for him the garden was a portrait of Babe Paley, the love of his life.

About two years later, Paley's office requested a second set of the photographs. Paley was trying to give the estate and, most importantly, the garden to the town of Manhasset to be used as a park, but the town turned down the gift. Ultimately the property passed through the hands of two developers, and the landscape was doomed.

The loss of the Paley garden, my first assignment, has always haunted me. I was alone in this marvelous landscape for quite a few days, eating my lunch by the pond, even sleeping on a soft grass path in the middle of the day when photography is impossible, and that experience has determined my course in life.

As the years passed and I traveled throughout the United States photographing gardens, I heard many similar stories of families and communities trying to save these ephemeral collaborations between man and nature. As this book clearly illustrates, we are now paying attention to these horticultural landmarks. I have been photographing them for more than a decade, working with five different cameras, two with film and three recording digitally as the technology has evolved over that period. We hope our mix of stories about these properties illustrates the diversity of groups at work preserving our landscape heritage today.

GARDENS TO VISIT

The Gardens of Alcatraz
Alcatraz Island
San Francisco, California 94133
www.alcatrazgardens.org

Ruth Bancroft Garden
1552 Bancroft Road
Walnut Creek, California 94598
www.ruthbancroftgarden.org

Bartram's Garden
54th Street and Lindbergh Boulevard
Philadelphia, Pennsylvania 19143
www.bartramsgarden.org

Blithewold Gardens
101 Ferry Road
Bristol, Rhode Island 02809
www.blithewold. org

Barnsley Gardens
Barnsley Gardens Road
Adairsville, Georgia 30103
www.barnsleyresort.com

Cummer Museum of Art and Gardens
829 Riverside Avenue
Jacksonville, Florida 32204
www.cummermuseum.org

The Fells
456 Route 103A
Newbury, New Hampshire 03255
www.thefells.org

Filoli
86 Canada Road
Woodside, California 94062
www.filoli.org

Pearl Fryar Topiary Garden
145 Broad Acres Road
Bishopville, South Carolina 29010
www.pearlfryar.com

Garland Farm
475 Bay View Drive
Bar Harbor, Maine 04609
www.beatrixfarrandsociety.org/
garland-farm/

Greenwood Gardens
274 Old Short Hills Road
Short Hills, New Jersey 07078
www.greenwoodgardens.org

Florence Griswold Museum
96 Lyme Street
Old Lyme, Connecticut 08637
www.flogris.org

Historic Deepwood Estate
1116 Mission Street SE
Salem, Oregon 97302
www.historicdeepwoodestate.org

Hollister House Garden
300 Nettleton Hollow Road
Washington, Connecticut 06793
www.hollisterhousegarden.org

Innisfree Garden
362 Tyrrel Road
Millbrook, New York 12545
www.innisfreegarden.org

The Kampong
4013 Douglas Road
Miami, Florida 33133
www.ntbg.org/gardens/kampong.
php

Ladew Topiary Gardens
3535 Jarrettsville Pike
Monkton, Maryland 21111
www.ladewgardens.com

Lotusland
695 Ashley Road
Santa Barbara, California 93108
www.lotusland.org

Madoo
618 Sagg Main Street,
Sagaponack, New York 11962
www.madoo.org

Middleton Place
4300 Ashley River Road
Charleston, South Carolina 29414
www.middletonplace.org

Minnesota Woman Suffrage Garden
State Capitol Mall
St. Paul, Minnesota 55155
www.mnhs.org/historic-sites/
minnesota-state-capitol

Moffatt-Ladd House and Garden
154 Market Street
Portsmouth, NH 03801
www.moffattladd.org

Montrose
320 Saint Mary's Road,
Hillsborough, North Carolina 27278
Email: montrosegdn@mac.com

William Paca House and Garden
99 Main Street
Annapolis, Maryland 21401
www.annapolis.org

Peckerwood Garden
20559 FM 359 Road
Hempstead, Texas 77445
www.peckerwoodgarden.com

Saint-Gaudens National Historic Site
139 Saint-Gaudens Road
Cornish, New Hampshire 03745
www.nps.gov/saga/

Anne Spencer Garden
1313 Pierce Street
Lynchburg, Virginia 24501
www.annespencermuseum.com

Anna Scripps Whitcomb Conservatory
876 Picnic Way
Detroit, Michigan 48207
www.belleisleconservancy.org

Untermyer Park and Gardens
945 North Broadway
Yonkers, New York 10701
www.untermyergardens.org

Yew Dell Botanical Gardens
6220 Old LaGrange Road
Crestwood, Kentucky 40014
www.yewdellgardens.org

Acknowledgments

First of all, we wish to thank all the owners, guardians, curators, and caretakers of the gardens in this book, who kindly allowed us to photograph their gardens and who provided us with essential information as to their history, rescue and preservation. Without their enormous help and generosity this book could not exist.

Others who provided vital background, general information, and hospitality were Valerie Aponik, Carolyn Hollenbeck, Lawrence Kreisman, James Madigan, Cara Montgomery, Annabelle Radcliffe-Trenner. Mary Reath found us the garden of Charles Richards on Great Wass Island. Anne Myers was enormously helpful with the Garden Club of America's archives in New York.

Curtice Taylor would like to thank Sam Gray, who has supported him in so many ways during the making of this book; May Brawley Hill, whose insights lit the way; Helen Pratt for helping get the project off the ground; Charles Birnbaum of the Cultural Landscape Foundation; Adams and Ruth Taylor, Christopher and Kathleen Taylor, Sally Barnet, Charles Duell, Blair Mathews, and Joseph Tringali for their hospitality; assistants Grant Gerber and Alexander Taylor; and Ryan Shorosky and Sofiya Brisker for their editing and digital skills.

We are especially grateful for the support of the New York Foundation for the Arts, whose grant enabled the project to come to fruition.

We would also like to thank Elizabeth White at The Monacelli Press, who patiently and carefully shepherded the book through its journey to publication, and Susan Evans of Design per se, whose elegant design has brought these gardens to life.

Library of Congress Control Number 2015938286

ISBN 9781580934084

Photographs by Curtice Taylor except as noted below:

Middleton Place: page 12 courtesy of Middleton Place

Anne Spencer Garden: pages 138, 141, 142, 143 © Jane Baber White;

page 140 courtesy of the Anne Spencer Foundation

Design: Susan Evans, Design per se

The Monacelli Press

236 West 27th Street, New York, New York 10001

www.monacellipress.com

Printed in China